THE TRUTH IS

1. Leveling up your craft to write a story that lives long after you've left the planet is what some might call a ridiculous goal.

2. You will not tell that story after reading just one how-to-write book.

3. You will not tell that story as the result of taking one seminar.

4. You know creating a timeless work of art will require the dedication of a world-class athlete. You will be training your mind with as much ferocity and single-minded purpose as an Olympic gold medal hopeful. That kind of cognitive regimen excites you, but you just haven't found a convincing storytelling dojo to do that work.

5. The path to leveling up your creative craft is a dark and treacherous one. You've been at it a long time, and it often feels like you're wearing three-dimensional horse blinders. More times than you'd like to admit, you're not sure if you're moving north or south or east or west. And the worst part? You can't see anyone else, anywhere, going through what you're going through. You're all alone.

WELCOME TO THE STORY GRID UNIVERSE
HERE'S HOW WE CONTEND WITH THOSE TRUTHS

1. We believe we find meaning in the pursuit of creations that last longer than we do. This is *not* ridiculous. Seizing opportunities and overcoming obstacles as we stretch ourselves to reach for seemingly unreachable creations is transformational. We believe this pursuit is the most valuable and honorable way to spend our time here. Even if— especially if—we never reach our lofty creative goals.

2. Writing just one story isn't going to take us to the top. We're moving from point A to Point A^{5000}. We've got lots of mountains to climb, lots of rivers and oceans to cross, and many deep dark forests to traverse along the way. We need topographic guides, and if they're not available, we'll have to figure out how to write them ourselves.

3. We're drawn to seminars to consume the imparted wisdom of an icon in the arena, but we leave with something far more valuable than the curriculum. We get to meet the universe's other pilgrims and compare notes on the terrain.

4. The Story Grid Universe has a virtual dojo, a university in which to work out and get stronger—a place to stumble, correct mistakes, and

stumble again, until the moves become automatic and mesmerizing to outside observers.

5. The Story Grid Universe has a performance space, a publishing house dedicated to leveling up the craft with clear boundaries of progress and the ancillary reference resources to pack for each project mission. There are an infinite number of paths to where you want to be, with a story that works. Seeing how others have made it down their own yellow-brick roads to release their creations into the timeless creative cosmos will help keep you on the straight and narrow path.

All are welcome—the more, the merrier. But please abide by the golden rule:

Put the work above all else, and trust the process.

THE MURDER OF ROGER ACKROYD BY AGATHA CHRISTIE

A STORY GRID MASTERWORK ANALYSIS GUIDE

SOPHIE THOMAS

Edited by
JAY PETERS

STORY GRID

STORY GRID

Story Grid Publishing LLC
223 Egremont Plain Road
PMB 191
Egremont, MA 01230

First Story Grid Publishing Paperback Edition
May 2021

For Information About Special Discount for Bulk Purchases,

Please visit www.storygridpublishing.com

Paperback ISBN: 978-1-64501-069-2
Ebook ISBN: 978-1-64501-134-7

For

All Past, Present, and Future Story Nerds

HOW TO READ THE MURDER OF ROGER ACKROYD BY AGATHA CHRISTIE: A STORY GRID MASTERWORK ANALYSIS GUIDE

1. Buy a copy of the novel and enjoy it without worrying about any of the Story Grid stuff.

2. Then, read each scene thinking about the Story Grid principles. Each scene is identified by a phrase that begins the scene and a phrase that ends the scene.

    a) At the conclusion of each scene is a section entitled *Analyzing the Scene*. By answering four Socratic questions, I'll walk you through how to determine the critical information for the Story Grid Spreadsheet—*Story Event* and *Value Shift*.

    b) Another section I've included at the end of each scene is "How the Scene Abides by the Five Commandments of Story-telling."

For each and every scene in *The Murder of Roger Ackroyd*, I indicate the Inciting Incident, Turning Point Progressive Complication, Crisis, Climax, and Resolution.

For those unfamiliar with Story Grid's Five Commandments of

Storytelling, you can read about them in the book *Story Grid 101* (free download on the Story Grid site), in *The Story Grid*: *What Good Editors Know*, or in articles about them on the site. Just access the "start here" or "resources" section of https://www.storygrid.com/ to read at your leisure.

c) In addition to the Story Grid Spreadsheet for *The Murder of Roger Ackroyd*, you can view the Story Grid Foolscap and the actual Story Grid Infographic at https://www.storygrid.com/masterwork/The-Murder-of-Roger-Ackroyd/.

INTRODUCTION

Why do we read Crime stories? And why do readers devour paperbacks with private eyes, cozy cat investigators, and amateur sleuths like Miss Marple? Why is Agatha Christie one of the best-selling authors of all time?

We read Crime for the *intrigue*, but what does that mean? We want to solve the case before the detective does. To satisfy that puzzle-solving drive, we have to make sense of complicated matters, and perhaps even escape the complications in our own lives for systematic, clue-based problems.

More specifically, when the detective exposes the criminal, we feel *intrigue, the core emotion of the genre,* as a kind of satisfaction when the clues finally add up and the characters' actions make sense.

Why Write a Murder Mystery?

Crime Story is a long-lasting genre with several subgenres to appeal to different readers. Often a reader gravitates toward a certain type of protagonist or antagonist; they may want to root for the criminal trying to avoid detection by the police (a caper), or for the professional or amateur detective attempting to expose a murderer. Some readers like a good courtroom debate.

The most popular subgenres change through time, but Crime stands as a widely consumed genre and appears in novels, TV, movies, and radio. Almost every form of media has a Crime segment because the audience for the genre is so large.

What hooks and powers us along this quest? Why have millions of people tuned into the *Law & Order* franchise every week since 1990? What has made Agatha Christie the best-selling novelist of all time, an author outsold only by William Shakespeare?[1]

Who Reads Murder Mysteries?

Are these the morbid dreams of the dark souls of outwardly nice people? Is the point of the Murder Mystery to teach people how to commit the perfect crime or to teach investigators how to catch the killer? Maybe. But let's back up and look at Crime Story from different angles.

Genre is simply a way to say, "Hey, reader, this is the kind of story you should expect out of this book." As a genre, Crime deals with the execution of one of the most core values to humans, *justice*. Without the trespass of justice, you have no crime. Crime stories dramatize events that move from justice to injustice and back again—or back to injustice. The reader is a spectator as the characters muddle through bringing justice back to their world. We love this as readers because we can participate in this quest without the threat to our personal lives.

As a society, we hunger for stories about the pursuit of justice. These books succeed from generation to generation to affirm our belief that justice can and will prevail, if even one person can outsmart the bad guys.

This satisfies one of our most primal needs—*security*.

We feel unsafe as we face plenty of crises of injustice in our daily lives. We encounter this from a distance on the news, closer to home through social media acquaintances, or in our own lives. It's impossible in this time to be sheltered from the evil in the world. The depth of the fear of injustice pervades our communities and has tainted those tasked with upholding the law.

We lose sleep over complicated problems without simple solutions. We sort through puzzles moment by moment.

In Murder Mysteries, we have capable—but imperfect—investigators working through the Red Herrings, testing every theory, and challenging assumptions. "Whodunnit?" is the question at the center of Crime Story—followed by "Why?" and "How?" We also want to participate in sorting out puzzle pieces and feel the core emotion of intrigue when it's over.

Crime Story writers must acknowledge the thirst for intrigue in their reader. The writer must hook the reader with its inciting incident —the crime.

The Inciting Crime is an obligatory moment in the story, and it is specific to the story's subgenre. The crime must be the perfect crime; there must be a true challenge to the core value of justice that seems impossible to solve. Don't bake in solutions to shield yourself from the challenge. Your readers will sniff out every one. Don't shield your characters from the evil of the world or from their own.

Are you about ready to quit here? I'm betting not. As a Crime Story writer, you are probably also driven by intrigue. Let that carry you to explore what your readers expect from a story of the genre.

As a Story Grid Certified Editor, I'm out to solve the mystery of "does this story work?" I look at a story from the vantage point of Editor's Six Core Questions to determine how it is working on the macro level. In this introductory material I will focus on the Murder Mystery subgenre. Even more specifically, I will look at the requirements of writing a Master Detective mystery, through the consummate Master Detective—Agatha Christie's Hercule Poirot.

After a high-level review of the big picture of the story, we'll dive into the scenes to see how Christie crafted powerful scenes that pull us forward to the surprising resolution. From these large and small component parts, she created the experience we all enjoy.

These inquiries will provide clues to help you understand the properties of a successful Murder Mystery like *The Murder of Roger Ackroyd*. The goal is to equip you to write your own bestseller. Let's dive into the Editor's Six Core Questions.

1. Olivia Rutigliano, "Agatha Christie Is the Best-Selling Novelist in History," *The Hub* (blog), *Literary* Hub, April 3, 2020, https://lithub.com/agatha-christie-is-the-best-selling-novelist-in-history/.

1) WHAT IS THE GENRE

You've got a character who breaks the law, a character who wants to figure it out, and twists and turns along the way. The primary forces of antagonism are *external*, meaning the protagonist is battling someone or something outside himself primarily. A character is pursuing justice and a criminal is pursuing injustice—or his own sense of justice, which is at odds with society's.

You've got a Crime story on your hands.

What kind of Crime story are you writing? While readers of Crime stories share a common interest in seeking intrigue and upholding the value of justice, we prefer different settings (such as a Historical Crime like *The Name of the Rose*), protagonists, inciting crimes (a heist, for example), and methods of investigation. Murder Mystery is one subgenre of Crime.

If you have a dead body, chances are you're writing a Murder Mystery.

SUBGENRES OF MURDER MYSTERY

Murder Mysteries themselves have sub-subgenres. What are the different types of Murder Mystery?

- **Master Detective:** This is where *The Murder of Roger Ackroyd* fits in. The Investigator character is the protagonist. Hercule Poirot, Holmes, and Columbo are all classic examples.
- **Cozy:** The protagonist/investigator is an untrained, charming character in a cozy environment, quite opposite of the Master Detective and Hardboiled investigator in every way. Christie's Miss Marple is an example of the amateur sleuth. She's a sweet grandmotherly type in whom people tend to confide trustingly. *Murder She Wrote's* Jessica Fletcher is the writer-turned-detective from an idyllic (but murderous) New England town. Angela Lansbury drew on Christie's Miss Marple character to create amateur detective Jessica Fletcher in the iconic Cozy TV series. A cat can even be a protagonist—and Cat Cozies have a strong following (e.g., *The Cat Who Could Read Backwards*). Other examples of cozy mystery sleuths include G.K. Chesterton's Father Brown, Dorothy Sayers's Lord Peter Wimsey, and Alan Bradley's Flavia de Luce.
- **Historical:** This is for the reader who wants to get lost in a historical time and place while solving the murder. *The Name of the Rose* by Umberto Eco and the Cadfael series by Ellis Peters are some masterworks to check out.
- **Noir/Hardboiled:** The protagonist is a cynical "antihero." If you're interested in these characters, *Double Indemnity* by James M. Cain may be your masterwork.
- **Paranormal:** There are paranormal characters and tropes, such as vampires and ghosts. The *True Blood* (Sookie Stackhouse) series is an example featuring vampires.
- **Police Procedural:** In this popular subgenre, the protagonists are the police detectives, as you find in the Vera Stanhope series by Ann Cleeves or Colin Dexter's Inspector Morse, as well as the *Law & Order* franchise.

Agatha Christie, the Queen of Mystery, has dominated the Cozy sub-subgenre with the Miss Marple mysteries *and* the Master Detective Murder Mystery sub-subgenre with her Hercule Poirot stories.

As we will see through the analysis, *The Murder of Roger Ackroyd* is a great example of the Master Detective subgenre for its many Red Herrings, its unreliable narrator accompanying Poirot in following the clues, and the surprising resolution in justice. All the while, we are in the capable hands of Hercule Poirot, as he challenges every detail that seems certain but uncorroborated through the retelling of the crime. The more certain we are that the clues fit neatly together, the more we find we are actually operating under the masterful redirection. When it seems as if a toddler has knocked our carefully constructed puzzle off the table and scattered all the pieces, we are actually closest to the truth as we pick up all the pieces and turn them back over. Assumptions are examined, witness statements and alibis are scrutinized, and clues are exposed for the Red Herrings they truly are.

Only a Master Detective can do this to satisfaction.

2) WHAT ARE THE CONVENTIONS AND OBLIGATORY MOMENTS OF THE CRIME GENRE?

The obligatory moments of any genre are scenes that have been so intricately woven into the DNA of the genre over thousands of years of storytelling that they define the genre. When a reader picks up a Love Story, she expects a lovers meet scene and a lovers' first kiss or intimate connection scene. These events must be on the page. If the writer promises in the course of the story that two people are going to fall in love, but they never have a moment when they run into each others' arms or send a passionate letter, the reader is going to be very disappointed.

Conventions are the conditions that set up the moments of change that are the obligatory moments. They are the setting, character, and catalysts that create the conditions for conflict that arise in the story.

Let's start with identifying the tried-and-true principles of the Murder Mystery.

CONVENTIONS OF A MURDER MYSTERY

These are setting, characters, and catalysts in the story that are specific to the genre and subgenre. You must add these items to set up your Murder Mystery.

MacGuffin. The MacGuffin is the criminal's tangible object of desire and why they commit the crime. In a Murder Mystery, the writer must wear both the protagonist's and the antagonist's hats, and the antagonist's want and need are most important to consider.

Sheppard's MacGuffin in *The Murder of Roger Ackroyd* is the letter from Mrs. Ferrars—the tangible evidence of his blackmail. He wants to get it from Roger Ackroyd and destroy it. He kills for that letter because it would expose his other crimes.

Red Herrings. These are seemingly revelatory false clues that mislead the protagonist-investigator. You have many opportunities to throw your reader and the investigator off.

- *Secrets.* All the characters keep secrets that can mislead the investigator. In *The Murder of Roger Ackroyd*, the secrets of the members of Ackroyd's household contribute to the complication and then resolution of the murder.
- *Characters.* The mysterious stranger becomes a convenient distraction for Sheppard, for example.
- *Alibis.* The alibis in *The Murder of Roger Ackroyd* help the police determine the time of death, but when Flora confesses she did not see her uncle that night, all alibis are worthless.
- *Timeline.* Colonel Blunt and Flora determine the time of death based on her lie and his assumption that he heard Ackroyd alive at 9:30 p.m. This is all a ruse.
- *Clues.* Legitimate clues can expose the truth, but Red Herrings cover it up. Examples in this story are footprints on the window sill, fingerprints on the dagger in Ackroyd's neck, and the infernal color of the boots or shoes Ralph wore on the night of the murder.
- Other examples: In *And Then There Were None*, one of the deaths is a Red Herring. The murderer must fake their own death to continue their quest for justice.

Villain Makes It Personal. The criminal's and the protagonist's objects of desire are mutually exclusive. The protagonist has a personal stake in solving the crime. The criminal wants to thwart the investigator, which could humiliate or destroy him. The criminal risks being exposed and being subject to justice. It's personal once the investigator is on the track. For Poirot, his intrinsic want is the truth. We see this character trait throughout his stories, and he states it directly multiple times—to the villain, no less!

Clock or Deadline. There is limited time for the protagonist and/or criminal to act. The clock gets started when Ackroyd invites Sheppard to dinner with the implication of an urgent private conversation. This puts Sheppard on alert that his secret may be out, so off stage he takes the day to prepare for the most extreme way out of his predicament— murder. That night, Sheppard has a tight window of time in which to murder Ackroyd, get back home for the phone call, and return to the house to remove the incriminating evidence and "discover" Ackroyd's dead body. Once Poirot accuses Sheppard, the master detective resets the clock and gives the criminal a deadline. Sheppard has until morning to take the "honorable" way out or he will be publicly accused to save Ralph.

Timeline. A key part of the investigative process involves who was where and when. What was the timeline of events? This is different from the ticking clock. Here, we're looking to the past. In essence, a Crime story has at least two story lines. One thread involves the crime itself with events from the past that are revealed out of chronological order. The investigation is another thread that unfolds in the story's present.

These first five are good Crime story rules of thumb. The following are specific to the Murder Mystery subgenre.

Clues. As Red Herrings are revealed and true clues are brought to light, the investigator can follow how the criminal progressed in their crime. Poirot follows the true progression of the clues in his summation and accusation of Sheppard.

Smoking Gun Clue. This term was coined by Sir Arthur Conan Doyle through the words of Holmes in *The Adventure of the Gloria Scott* (1893). A conclusive bit of evidence seals the fate of the scapegoat and/or criminal because it helps the investigator make sense of the crime.

Stock Characters:

Investigative character. The type of investigator is specific to the particular sub-subgenre of Murder Mystery. Poirot and Holmes are the archetypal Master Detectives, in that they remain apart from the police, the amateur, and the criminal. Thanks to Watson, Hastings, and Sheppard here, the master detective remains aloof, and their movements and investigations can remain off the page in places where mystery is needed. In a Cat Cozy, it's the titular cat. But the detective in a Murder Mystery can be a police officer (*Law & Order*), private investigator (the Kinsey Millhone novels), or amateur sleuth (Miss Marple or Jessica Fletcher). The cast of characters in *And Then There Were None* all act as sleuths as they try to save their lives. They also all act as antagonists to each other. Christie introduces the official investigator only in the epilogue when the criminal confesses in a letter to him.

Watson/sidekick. The sidekick assists the investigative character in solving the crime and builds them up as the brilliant mind. Clearly, the role is derived from Doyle's Dr. John Watson, who assisted and narrated for Holmes. Christie's Captain Hastings is the typical sidekick for Poirot, but in *The Murder of Roger Ackroyd*, Hastings is replaced by Sheppard. It was brilliant because having Poirot's ear invariably signals innocence to the reader. *But notice Christie did not do away with the sidekick character convention.*

Sidekicks perform different functions for the detective, but more importantly, the sidekick helps the writer solve several problems that arise in writing the story. The Watson role is the detective's sounding board. With an assistant to discuss the case, the reader is spared too many scenes of internal dialogue and repetitive narration. We're introduced to clues, alibis, motives, and other conventional details through their conversation. It's true that Holmes and Poirot are too busy, too eccentric, and too self-absorbed to narrate their own stories, but shielding the reader from their theory of the case maintains the mystery.

Criminal. Without the criminal there would be no crime, no challenge to justice, and no story.

Victim. The slain, a scapegoat, and/or someone being pursued by the criminal.

OBLIGATORY MOMENTS OF A MURDER MYSTERY

Obligatory moments are specific moments of change within the story that shift the genre's core value, in this case justice, for the better or worse. All scenes must make it more or less likely that the criminal will be exposed and justice restored. But these are special moments within all Crime stories that readers of the genre are looking for. They include unexpected events, revelations, decisions, and actions.

1. **Dead Body Scene.** You must have a murder to have a Murder Mystery. This is the *inciting crime* specific to the Murder Mystery subgenre. All Crime stories require an inciting crime that engages the reader's intrigue, threatens their intrinsic sense of justice, and sets off the investigation.

The Murder of Roger Ackroyd has *three* dead bodies. The story opens with the suspected suicide of Mrs. Ferrars. Though there are questions of justice surrounding Mrs. Ferrars's death, that isn't the inciting crime of the story. We find out that her husband, the late Mr. Ferrars, died the year before under suspicious circumstances. But the inciting Dead Body scene is when Roger Ackroyd is found murdered in his locked study. That's when the investigation commences. That's when the suspects start acting shady.

That's when Poirot gets involved.

2. **Speech in Praise of the Villain.** At some point, one or more characters must make a statement admiring the cunning of the criminal. Poirot, confident in his own skills, is willing to own that his opponent is almost his match in plotting. Poirot several times admits the complexity of the case. This obligatory moment demands the investigator change their tactics to catch a worthy adversary. Poirot paints a descriptive picture of the murderer in scene 17, deciding the appeal to the group did not work and now he must investigate largely apart from Sheppard.

This doesn't have to be the cliché Bond villain monologue, and it can be given by the protagonist, the villain himself, or other characters.

3. **Discovery of MacGuffin.** Why did the murderer commit the murder? This is part of Poirot's summation at the very end. He finally pinpoints it when accusing Sheppard. Sheppard himself drops breadcrumbs early and often. The letter confessing the blackmailer's name

(which disappears) gives the villain's motive, but then drops out of the storyline.

4. Following the Clues. This is the quest of the Middle Build or about the middle 50 percent of the story. This is the core investigation. The recent film adaptation of *Murder on the Orient Express* (2017) shows the buildup of clues on a moving/snow-trapped train and how the accumulation of clues only complicates the case further.

In *Murder of Roger Ackroyd*, the clues are intentionally designed by the murderer to lead the police to frame a scapegoat. The police fall into the murder's trap. When Flora Ackroyd hires Hercule Poirot, he turns up the heat on the criminal because he follows a different method and is not distracted by the Red Herrings (false and misleading clues). He calls out the suspects' secrets; nefarious or innocent, they must all be brought to light to clear up the case. As motives emerge, alibis are shattered, and other clues compound on each other, the case gets murkier and murkier. Only Poirot can see his way through it.

5. Exposure of the Criminal. This is the Murder Mystery's core event. The readers have diligently followed the clues and kept pace with the detective, all for this moment. Naturally, this typically comes at the end. In *The Murder of Roger Ackroyd*, Christie employs her classic grand summation. The investigator gathers all the suspects together and moves suspect to suspect, tying up all the loose ends, exonerating each one by one, until only the guilty party is left. After mapping out to the whole group how he arrived at his theory of the crime, Poirot then reveals to only Sheppard the murderer's identity—Dr. Sheppard himself—giving him an opportunity to confess.

In Christie's *And Then There Were None* (which she called the most difficult she ever wrote), the exposure of the criminal comes *after* the Brought to Justice moment, which is typically the story's resolution. The suspects are killed one by one on an island, with no escape. The revelation comes through a posthumous letter from the killer to the investigator, who finds a scene of ten dead bodies—the murderer is among them.

6. Brought to Justice or Escapes Justice. This moment resolves the story. The Murder Mystery must end up with justice, injustice, or irony. The bad guy gets caught, is arrested/eliminated, or is identified but gets away with it. This is obligatory because an unresolved cliffhanger cheats the audience. *The Murder of Roger Ackroyd* ends in the form of justice best suited to the story. After telling the whole story to Poirot, Sheppard takes his own life to spare his sister the distress of knowing his crimes.

Many of today's Murder Mysteries conclude with a more ironic ending, in which justice is served nominally, but a deeper injustice scars the protagonist or society. Sometimes the victim is truly the villain, and the murderer is the hero in the wider lens of society. The murderer of *And Then There Were None* takes the law into his own hands as he kills off murderers who are guilty by proxy. Is it legal? No. But the balance of Justice is restored through the elimination of ten remorseless criminals who would never be convicted for their crimes. Poirot allows a poetic justice to reign in *Murder on the Orient Express* as the murdered man's victims together premeditate and commit the murder.

3) WHAT IS THE POINT OF VIEW AND NARRATIVE DEVICE?

A big decision the writer of any story must make is *who* is telling the story? In a Murder Mystery, the writer must pay particular attention to how much the reader knows relative to the characters in the story, and that means choosing the narrator wisely.

Christie's Hercule Poirot mysteries are typically narrated by the "Watson" character, most often Captain Hastings. He's Poirot's champion and the bumbling, well-intentioned sidekick. He tells the story in first person. This gives Christie the opportunity to keep Poirot elevated as the brilliant egotist. Poirot keeps his cards close to his chest, and Hastings tries to draw him out and guess at the master detective's theories. Hastings also helps Poirot figure out certain clues by making offhand remarks that spark Poirot's "voilà!" (Doyle's Sherlock Holmes stories are narrated in the same way.)

In *The Murder of Roger Ackroyd*, Christie uses a Watson character to narrate the story's events in first-person point of view. This time, she innovated it by making the narrator the murderer. The narrative device is Sheppard's journal, which he reveals was meant to be the story of Poirot's failure. When you reread the story, you can see Christie never cheats in Sheppard's unreliable account. She accomplishes this brilliantly by having Sheppard omit his reactions and use *double entendre* in his observations. His journal (and therefore the story) reads differently depending on your perspective as a reader.

What are some other options available to writers of Crime stories? For the tough task of killing off all her characters in *And Then There Were None*, Christie employed a third-person omniscient narrator with moments of *free indirect style*. When a particular character is on the chopping block, Christie allows a peek into the mind to experience their fear and guilt and paranoia. The final revelation comes in the epilogue in the form of a first-person letter from the murderer. However, some readers might find that to be a cheap trick of tying up loose ends, a form of *deus ex machina* that gives the power to the investigator. It worked for Christie, but it might not work again.

Sir Arthur Conan Doyle combines the first-person narrative of Watson with the third-person reportage of the murderer in *A Study in Scarlet*. Doyle divides the story into two parts. The first part, narrated by Watson, chronicles his steps along with Holmes until the detective masterfully brings in the criminal. The second is the back story, told in part by third-person reportage (the oft-used flashback scene), before returning to Watson's first-person observations, as Holmes shares his process.

A note about Narrative Drive. This term describes the primary engine that compels someone to continue reading to the end of the story. It involves the amount of information characters have in relation to the readers and the questions that keep them engaged. The writer has to make this choice. As Shawn Coyne says, "The writer is in the power position in the Reader/Writer/Character triangle."[1] You decide when and how to dispense information to your characters and your readers. There are three forms of narrative drive.[2]

Mystery is when the characters know more than the reader. This is typical of detective stories like the Poirot and Miss Marple series where the investigator is trying to sort out characters' secrets.

Suspense happens when the reader and protagonist possess the same amount of information about the crime. Alan Bradley's Flavia de Luce mysteries are driven by suspense, and readers solve the crime along with the young amateur detective.

Dramatic Irony is giving the reader information that the protagonist does not have. At the end of Louise Penny's first Armand Gamache mystery *Still Life,* Clara Morrow steps into the house of the killer. We (the readers) know she's about to confront the killer, but she does not. The tension ramps up through the conversation with an unnamed man, who then attacks her. But only in the next scene do we realize it is not who we suspected.

---

1. Shawn Coyne, "Narrative Drive," *What it Takes* (blog) 14 June 2013, http://www.stevenpressfield.com/2013/06/narrative-drive-2/ retrieved 5 January 2018.
2. For an excellent series on narrative drive, see Valerie Francis, "Writing a Page Turner Part 1," Story Grid (blog) November 30, 2018, https://storygrid.com/writing-a-page-turner-part-1/.

4) WHAT IS THE OBJECT OF DESIRE?

Objects of desire are the wants (conscious) and needs (unconscious) of the protagonist and antagonist.

Crime stories play on our basic need for *security*. The criminal (usually) has a very specific motive for committing the murder, but generally there are common objects of desire for these character types. The criminal wants his own sense of security, that is, to get away with murder. The protagonist (usually the investigator) seeks to restore security to the world by bringing the criminal to justice.

In *The Murder of Roger Ackroyd*, Poirot states his objective quite clearly: "I mean to know the truth." When Flora hires him to exonerate Ralph, Poirot warns her that he will stop at nothing until justice is served, even if the outcome is unfavorable to her. He makes it clear that his debt is not to her but to justice. His need is to have security and order in his new town.

Sheppard *wants* to protect himself from prosecution. His motive for murder is to cover up his blackmail of Mrs. Ferrars. He blackmailed her for financial security because he was (or perceives he was) the victim of an investment scheme. Acting on his *want* leads to injustice and then tyranny, as he murders Ackroyd, frames someone who sees him as a best friend, and causes unrest in his community. What Sheppard really *needs* is to see that he can't victimize other people. He states in his apologia that his purpose in narrating the case was to one day publish the story of Poirot's one failure. However, Poirot gives him an ultimatum. "Sacrifice yourself for the good of your sister." This awakens Sheppard's *need* for atonement, which he has been subverting by victimizing other people and covering his own weakness.

Poirot, the enactor of justice, is the protagonist. And with the Story Grid Spreadsheet we track his pursuit of justice throughout the story.

We tend to connect with the narrator of a story, however, and we feel drawn to Sheppard's side of things. We assume he and Poirot want the same thing. As we creep closer to justice and the mystery gets clearer, Sheppard's danger increases. Their goals are in direct opposition until the end when Sheppard realizes what he needs.

Your protagonist and villain must have clear wants and needs. The dedicated Murder Mystery reader will never be satisfied by a criminal with no clear reason to commit murder. The revelation of the *why* is as important in the exposure of the criminal moment as the *how*. Sheppard is an excellent choice for the criminal in *The Murder of Roger Ackroyd* because he seems to have no reason to be suspected. But when it's revealed that *he* is Mrs. Ferrars's blackmailer, all the pieces click into place. He not only has a *how*, but he has a *why*.

5) WHAT IS THE CONTROLLING IDEA OF THE STORY?

The controlling idea of a story, also known as a theme, tells you the value at stake and whether it will resolve positively or negatively. It does this by revealing the result or change in the story and the cause or reason for it. How does life change for the characters in a Murder Mystery? At the beginning, the characters are alive, and by the end at least one is dead. But life-and-death isn't the value we're tracking. Over the course of the story, justice is trespassed, and then at the end it is either restored (positive), left unjust (negative), or ends in irony.

So what is the nature of the value at stake in the global story when a murder is committed?

The characters experience injustice—whether or not they care for the victim. (As it turns out, Ackroyd is not really missed that much.) If not for vengeance for the dead, often the characters desire justice either to avoid wrongful conviction, protect their community, or just restore the sense of balance.

As the investigator works out the mystery, he aims to restore justice. So the story plugs along a spectrum of value that includes justice as the most positive and tyranny as the most negative.

Justice ++
Unfairness +

Equilibrium ~
Injustice -
Tyranny - -

Keep in mind, the polarities expressed here (e.g., + or -) describe these values relative to one another on the global value spectrum. Within the scene analysis and in the spreadsheet, I'll track the polarity shifts as movement toward the positive or negative end of the spectrum.

We have a sense of justice and injustice, but what about the other values?

Tyranny is the negation of the negation of this value. Tyranny reigns when the perpetrator runs the show by escaping justice and pulling the strings within society. The state of life in a Crime story doesn't have to actually reach tyranny, but the potential for tyranny and the vehicle for it must be expressed and must exist. That means there's a threat from a powerful force to make and change the rules on a whim, leaving the population unsafe. The darkest point of a Murder Mystery is when the perpetrator seems to get away with their crimes. In our text, it's when Sheppard has so perfectly framed his friend Ralph and Ursula Paton, with their trusting cooperation, that only his own confession will save them and the people of King's Abbot from tyranny. Failing to bring the criminal to justice goes beyond the individual. If Poirot can't stop the villains, they win. There can be no justice—only tyranny.

Unfairness is a more positive value because it is a move toward justice. The crime has been committed, the suspect is at large, but the investigator is working to shed light on the case. Being realistic, there's always unfairness in the world. A population's sense of safety depends on a certain amount of unfairness. As my fellow Story Grid editor Anne Hawley says, "We feel safer at home not because every crime is perfectly punished but because we see that some crimes are—that good men and women are at work seeking criminals and sometimes putting them behind bars."

How does this story end? A telegram arrives, allowing Poirot to corner Sheppard. Sheppard confesses and then kills himself. The murderer is exposed (to the relevant people) and eliminated. It ends positively but with irony.

No, Sheppard is not brought to legal justice. But the debt to society is paid with Sheppard's death. The community doesn't really need his confession or trial. They need Ralph to be exonerated and for life to go on (with all the benefits of Ackroyd's death). The murderer is not dangerous to anyone else. Poirot, having been softened from his earlier straight-edge character, is satisfied with an outcome that doesn't destroy Caroline, Sheppard's sister—another innocent victim.

Justice prevails.

How does the value of justice change throughout the novel?

At the beginning of the story, Mrs. Ferrars has killed herself. On the surface, there is a sense of *equilibrium*: her life for a life (her husband's). We move from this equilibrium to injustice when Roger Ackroyd is murdered for his proximity to Mrs. Ferrars and the threat he poses to Sheppard. Throughout the story, we move up the spectrum toward justice as Poirot gets a better sense of the *how*, *why*, and *who* behind the murder. We move toward injustice and even tyranny as the case becomes more complicated and Ralph becomes more embroiled in the murder. Until Poirot can prove the culpability of the murderer, the potential for tyranny looms.

So, we need a vehicle for justice. This is why people read Crime stories—to go along the trail to justice with the investigator. The *how* we get from equilibrium to injustice to tyranny and to justice evokes the core emotion of *intrigue* in the reader.

Poirot's systematic investigation—his iconic order and method—propels the reader to the final solution. He follows clues, interviews suspects, and employs his "little grey cells" to solve the mystery.

A controlling idea for *The Murder of Roger Ackroyd* could be: Justice prevails when Poirot methodically solves the murder of Ackroyd, and his murderer is identified and eliminated.

6) WHAT IS THE BEGINNING HOOK, MIDDLE BUILD, AND ENDING PAYOFF?

Identifying the beginning hook, middle build, and ending payoff of the story are important steps of the editing process. Every writer should try to answer this question when staring at their first draft: "Can I boil down my three movements into one sentence each?" Use the simplest terms possible. Don't get hung up on the progressive complications at this stage. Those details come later.

Agatha Christie's three-sentence summary might look like this:

- Beginning Hook: Roger Ackroyd is murdered.
- Middle Build: Hercule Poirot investigates.
- Ending Payoff: Hercule Poirot catches the murderer and brings him to justice.

Yes, this may be a pretty generic story line for any Murder Mystery. But this is crucial to identify the essence of each movement, as if you're recommending a book you loved to a friend.

We can expand this to the global Five Commandments of Story-telling to get a more detailed sense of the big picture.

- Inciting Incident: Roger Ackroyd is murdered.
- Turning Point Progressive Complication: Flora Ackroyd

admits she lied about seeing Roger Ackroyd at 9:30 p.m., forcing the police to start over.

- Crisis: Will Sheppard confess to the murder and spare Ralph Paton?
- Climax: Poirot gives Sheppard twenty-four hours to take his own life or be arrested.
- Resolution: Sheppard confesses in his written account and plans to overdose on Veronal, just as Mrs. Ferrars did in response to his blackmail.

But suppose you want to break the story into smaller parts. You can apply the Five Commandments of Storytelling to the beginning hook, middle build, and ending payoff.

BEGINNING HOOK

While the murder doesn't occur until scene 5, the stage is set in the first scene with Mrs. Ferrars's suicide.

- Inciting Incident: Roger Ackroyd is murdered.
- Turning Point: Flora Ackroyd hires Hercule Poirot.
- Crisis: Will Poirot come out of retirement to investigate or leave it to the police?
- Climax: Poirot takes the case.
- Resolution: Without enough evidence, Raglan seeks to arrest Ralph Paton.

MIDDLE BUILD

The middle build follows Poirot's investigation as he works separately from the police. He pursues each character's claims about that night of the murder, and when they continue to be untruthful, he digs into their personal lives to find their motives.

- Inciting Incident: Poirot begins to investigate with Sheppard apart from the police.

- Turning Point Progressive Complication: Poirot promises to find everyone's secrets.
- Crisis: Will Poirot see through the Red Herrings and determine the true course of events?
- Climax: Flora admits she lied about seeing her uncle that night.
- Resolution: Poirot plants a story about Ralph's arrest.

ENDING PAYOFF

At this point, Poirot is certain of most of the facts of the case. He is waiting on a last piece of evidence. Off the page, he has found Ralph, discovered the secrets of the group, and landed on Sheppard as his suspect. The ending payoff is kicked off by Poirot's regathering of the group. Notice there is a gathering of the suspects in each act—the dinner party on the night of the murder; Poirot's plea for information about Ralph's whereabouts, and Poirot's summation.

- Inciting Incident: Poirot arranges a reunion of the suspects.
- Turning Point: A telegram arrives with the truth of Sheppard's phone call.
- Crisis: Will Dr. Sheppard confess to the murder or let Ralph take the fall?
- Climax: Dr. Sheppard denies Poirot's accusation.
- Resolution: Dr. Sheppard, finally convicted by his conscience, takes his own life.

WHY IS THE MURDER OF ROGER ACKROYD A MASTERWORK OF THE MURDER MYSTERY SUBGENRE?

Why was this particular Christie novel voted the best crime novel *ever* by the Crime Writers' Association in 2013?[1]

Hercule Poirot's defeat of Sheppard is sound because he keeps him close throughout the investigation, lulling Sheppard into believing his own ruse. Instead of delivering justice himself, Poirot awakens Sheppard's need to *restore justice himself* by appealing to Sheppard's humanity in saving his sister. The narrative device of antagonist-narrator is masterful as the ultimate Red Herring. On a large scale, the story is successful, intriguing, and innovative.

The Editor's Six Core Questions and the Story Grid Foolscap give you guidance about the macro level of the story. You'll also find the Infographic, which plots the overall movement of the value at stake. Now, let's dive into the micro level. I've filled out the Story Grid spreadsheet to organize my analysis. Grab your Story Grid spreadsheet that you've filled out after you read *The Murder of Roger Ackroyd* and compare notes.

THE FIVE COMMANDMENTS OF STORYTELLING

1. Inciting Incident: An event, causal or circumstantial, that throws the central character of a scene out of homeostasis.

- Causal: An action by a character.
- Coincidental: An event out of the control of the characters, e.g., the weather.

2. Progressive Complications: Conflict that makes life more and more complicated for the character(s).

Turning Point Progressive Complication: The precise progressive complication that shifts the value from positive to negative, negative to positive, (or bad to worse/good to better). The turning point can be either:

- Active: An event, an action, sparks the character to a crisis. Example: Ralph Paton, the missing man, walks into the room.
- Revelatory: A revelation sparks the character to a crisis. "Luke, I am your father."

3. Crisis: A dilemma the character faces.

- Best Bad Choice: The character must sort through two unfavorable outcomes and choose the lesser of two (or more) evils.
- Irreconcilable Goods: What is good for one is not good for another. When presented with options that could benefit him or another, he must choose one.

4. Climax: The character's choice at his/her crisis point. This includes the decision and the action taken.

5. Resolution: The aftermath of the character's choice (climax). This is how the rest of the scene plays out.

To solve the mystery of how to make this story work, let's look at the scenes one by one.

Note: I have chosen to analyze each chapter as a scene except where Christie indicates them herself (e.g., chapter 4 is broken into scenes 4 and 5). These make for longer scenes, with many beats and progressive complications. You could certainly make a case for multiple scenes in a chapter. However, we will view the scenes like this to show the progression of the investigation in the simplest terms.

---

1. Jonathan Brown, "*Agatha Christie's The Murder of Roger Ackroyd voted best crime novel ever,*" *The Independent*, 5 November 2013, https://www.independent.co.uk/arts-entertainment/books/news/agatha-christie-s-murder-roger-ackroyd-voted-best-crime-novel-ever-8923395.html, (retrieved 4 January 2018). "The survey, of members of the Crime Writers' Association (CWA) of professional novelists, concluded that Christie's 1926 mystery *The Murder of Roger Ackroyd* was the finest example of the genre ever penned."

THE MURDER OF ROGER
ACKROYD

ACT I: THE BEGINNING HOOK

ROGER ACKROYD IS MURDERED

CHAPTER 1: DR SHEPPARD AT THE BREAKFAST TABLE

SCENE 1

1425 words

"Mrs. Ferrars died on the ... got up from the table."

Summary: Our narrator, James Sheppard, the village doctor of King's Abbot, returns to the home he shares with his sister, Caroline, after a house call. Mrs. Ferrars has been discovered dead of a Veronal overdose. Caroline already knows the situation, having been informed through a gossip-chain of servants. Caroline theorizes that Mrs. Ferrars's "accidental" overdose was actually a suicide, motivated by remorse for poisoning her husband a year before. Sheppard is worried by Mrs. Ferrars's death and impatient with Caroline's theories.

ANALYZING THE SCENE

STORY EVENT

A Story Event is an active change of a universal human value for one or more characters as a result of conflict (one character's desires clash with another's, or an environmental shift changes the value positively or negatively).

A Working Scene contains at least one Story Event. To determine a scene's Story Event, answer these four Socratic questions:

1. What are the characters literally doing—that is, what are their micro on-the-surface actions?

Sheppard returns home from confirming Mrs. Ferrars's overdose death. He reluctantly discusses it with his sister, Caroline.

2. What is the essential tactic of the characters—that is, what above-the-surface macro behaviors are they employing that are linked to a universal human value?

Caroline airs her theory that Mrs. Ferrars killed herself out of guilt for having murdered her husband a year before (another theory). Sheppard lets slip that he also considered it (he had looked for a letter of confession) but then angrily denies it.

3. What beyond-the-surface universal human values have changed for one or more characters in the scene? Which one of those value changes is most important and should be included in the Story Grid Spreadsheet?

Sheppard is "upset and worried" at Mrs. Ferrars's death. By the end of the scene, Caroline's theories have moved him to anger.

We highlight the value that best tracks the scene-by-scene progress of the global value at stake. In a Murder Mystery, the universal human value shifts that prompt the murderer to action are important. We'll follow Sheppard's value shift in much of the Beginning Hook.

Worry to Fear (-/ - -)

4. The Scene Event Synthesis: What Story Event sums up the scene's on-the-surface, above-the-surface, and beyond-the-surface change? We will enter that event in the Story Grid Spreadsheet.

Mrs. Ferrars has died. Sheppard shuts down Caroline's theories of murder-suicide.

HOW THE SCENE ABIDES BY THE FIVE COMMANDMENTS OF STORYTELLING

Inciting Incident: Causal. Mrs. Ferrars has died of an overdose.

Progressive Complication: Caroline theorizes that Mrs. Ferrars killed herself out of guilt for murdering her husband.

Turning Point Progressive Complication: Active. Caroline baits Sheppard to get information—"Ten to one she left a letter confessing everything."

Crisis: Best bad choice. Ignoring Caroline will do no good. Responding to her bait will encourage her theories.

Climax: "There was no letter!" This shows Caroline that Sheppard also considered suicide.

Resolution: Caroline is triumphant. Sheppard leaves the table, angry.

NOTES

- Foreshadowing: "I'm not going to pretend that at the moment I foresaw the events of the next few weeks. I emphatically did not do so."
- Christie subtly references Sheppard's guilt, but expertly redirects the reader's attention. Why would he be "upset and worried" as a doctor to discover a death?

- Mrs. Ferrars's death is an unexpected event that throws the whole village out of homeostasis, particularly Sheppard and Ackroyd, but it's not the story's inciting incident. Although there is some mystery concerning the circumstances of her death, it is established that she died by suicide.
- Convention: *Dead body*

CHAPTER 2: WHO'S WHO IN KING'S ABBOT
SCENE 2

2381 words

"Before I proceed further with ... or something of the kind."

Summary: The first eleven paragraphs comprise exposition to acquaint the reader with the village and its inhabitants, particularly Roger Ackroyd and Mrs. Ferrars, the village's VIPs who own the two big houses. Ackroyd and Mrs. Ferrars were rumored to be engaged. Sheppard runs into Ackroyd, who urgently needs to speak with him. Sheppard agrees to come over for dinner that night. Miss Gannett then pumps the doctor for information.

Once he returns to his surgery, Miss Russell is waiting for him.

ANALYZING THE SCENE

STORY EVENT

A Story Event is an active change of a universal human value for one or more characters as a result of conflict (one character's desires clash with another's, or an environmental shift changes the value positively or negatively).

A Working Scene contains at least one Story Event. To determine a scene's Story Event, answer these four Socratic questions:

1. What are the characters literally doing—that is, what are their micro on-the-surface actions?

Sheppard muses over the gossip surrounding Mrs. Ferrars on his daily doctor's rounds. He has a premonition of foreboding. Ackroyd invites him to dinner to discuss urgent matters. Miss Russell asks Sheppard about drug addiction and untraceable poisons.

2. What is the essential tactic of the characters—that is, what above-the-surface macro behaviors are they employing that are linked to a universal human value?

Sheppard fears Mrs. Ferrars has told Ackroyd or Ralph Paton about the blackmail. Miss Russell seeks information from Ackroyd to help her son. Miss Gannett wants the gossip on Mrs. Ferrars first.

3. What beyond-the-surface universal human values have changed for one or more characters in the scene? Which one of those value changes is most important and should be included in the Story Grid Spreadsheet?

We'll track the value for Sheppard in this scene. His memory of Mrs. Ferrars and Ralph together brings over him a sense of *foreboding*.
Reminiscent (~) to Foreboding (-)

4. The Scene Event Synthesis: What Story Event sums up the scene's on-the-surface, above-the-surface, and beyond-the-surface change? We will enter that event in the Story Grid Spreadsheet.

Sheppard fears Mrs. Ferrars has told someone about the blackmail. Ackroyd invites Sheppard to dinner.

HOW THE SCENE ABIDES BY THE FIVE COMMANDMENTS OF STORYTELLING

Inciting Incident: Causal. Sheppard goes about his daily rounds.

Turning Point Progressive Complication: Active. Ackroyd approaches Sheppard with an urgent update on Mrs. Ferrars, saying, "It's worse than you know."

Crisis: Best bad choice. Should Sheppard abandon his rounds to speak with Ackroyd now? Should he meet with Ackroyd later? (How time sensitive is this conversation? How dangerous is it to Sheppard?)

Climax: Sheppard postpones their conversation and accepts Ackroyd's invitation to dinner.

Resolution: Sheppard returns to his appointments at his surgery and receives Miss Russell, Ackroyd's housekeeper.

NOTES

- There are four distinct *beats* in the first half of the chapter— Sheppard's exposition of the residents of King's Abbot; Ackroyd and Sheppard's conversation; Miss Gannett and Sheppard's (reported) conversation; and Miss Russell's appointment—but altogether, the *scene* as a whole paints a picture of King's Abbot and the ominous impact of Mrs. Ferrars's death. Weaving these beats together in one scene, Christie shows her expertise at dropping breadcrumbs, creating suspense, and redirecting the reader.
- Convention: *Red Herrings*. Miss Russell asks about untraceable poisons.

- Convention: *Clock*. A convention of the Murder Mystery, the clock starts when Ackroyd seems desperate to speak to Sheppard. He has until dinner at 7:30 p.m. to plan his crime.

CHAPTER 3: THE MAN WHO GREW VEGETABLE MARROWS

SCENE 3

3280 words

"I told Caroline at lunch ... to play a lone hand."

Summary: Sheppard meets his neighbor, Hercule Poirot, without knowing his profession. Sheppard reveals to Poirot that he lost a large inheritance in a gamble. Caroline told Ackroyd about Ralph's being in King's Abbot and believes he went straight to the inn to find him. She overheard a conversation between Ralph and a mysterious girl, in which Ralph said his stepfather was going to cut him off "without a shilling."

ANALYZING THE SCENE

STORY EVENT

A Story Event is an active change of a universal human value for one or more characters as a result of conflict (one character's desires clash with another's, or an environmental shift changes the value positively or negatively).

A Working Scene contains at least one Story Event. To determine a scene's Story Event, answer these four Socratic questions:

1. What are the characters literally doing—that is, what are their micro on-the-surface actions?

Sheppard meets his new neighbor. He talks with Caroline and Poirot about Ralph. Ralph hides from his stepfather at the Three Boars Inn. Sheppard risks a visit with Ralph.

2. What is the essential tactic of the characters—that is, what above-the-surface macro behaviors are they employing that are linked to a universal human value?

Sheppard is relieved that Ralph doesn't know anything of his blackmail. Sheppard realizes Ralph could be set up to take the fall for Ackroyd's murder. Ralph is concerned about his stepfather but refuses help.

3. What beyond-the-surface universal human values have changed for one or more characters in the scene? Which one of those value changes is most important and should be included in the Story Grid Spreadsheet?

Let's track the value for Sheppard in this scene. He starts to hatch his plot to murder Ackroyd and incriminate Ralph—two birds with one stone.

Desperate (-) to Plotting (--)

4. The Scene Event Synthesis: What Story Event sums up the scene's on-the-surface, above-the-surface, and beyond-the-surface change? We will enter that event in the Story Grid Spreadsheet.

Sheppard meets Poirot and visits Ralph, who is in trouble with his stepfather, Roger Ackroyd.

HOW THE SCENE ABIDES BY THE FIVE COMMANDMENTS OF STORYTELLING

Inciting Incident: Coincidental. Sheppard's neighbor ("Mr. Porrott") hits Sheppard with a vegetable marrow thrown over the fence.

Progressive Complications: Sheppard meets Poirot. Sheppard reveals having "risked the substance for the shadow." Poirot, a stranger, is in Ackroyd's confidence. Ralph is engaged to Flora.

Turning Point Progressive Complication: Revelatory. Caroline overheard Ralph talking about disliking his stepfather but needing his money when he "pops off."

Crisis: Best bad choice. To call on Ralph at the Three Boars or not? Sheppard isn't sure how he will be received by Ralph, since his "earnest *tête-à-tête*" with Mrs. Ferrars the day before she died. But in the event that Mrs. Ferrars did confide in him, Sheppard must know if he can do anything with him (i.e., bribe him, incriminate him, or worse).

Climax: Sheppard calls on Ralph.

Resolution: Ralph receives him with no indication of knowing about the blackmail. Ralph reveals the trouble with his stepfather and his need to "play a lone hand."

NOTES

- Sheppard reveals his weakness for greed in conversation with Poirot: "I was foolish—and worse than foolish—*greedy*. I risked the substance for the shadow." (Emphasis added.)
- Ralph Paton unknowingly makes himself Sheppard's scapegoat with the conversation Caroline overheard in the

woods and the ominous threat to Ackroyd, "I've got to play a lone hand." He has a motive for murder when it is revealed that he's in big trouble. His stepfather will most likely cut him off without a cent, and his stepfather is presumably on his way to see him in a tirade.

- Convention: *Red Herring.* "I've got to play a lone hand."

CHAPTER 4: DINNER AT FERNLY

PART I: SCENE 4

1926 words

"It was just a few ... relapsed into his usual taciturnity."

Summary: Sheppard arrives at Fernly Park for dinner and meets the house members, guests, and servants. As he wanders the house before dinner, Sheppard notices that Miss Russell has a flimsy justification for being in the drawing room and seems to be out of breath. He hears the sound of the silver table lid closing. Flora and Mrs. Ackroyd, Roger Ackroyd's widowed sister-in-law, confirm the news of Flora's engagement. They sit down to dinner. Ackroyd is depressed and miserable.

ANALYZING THE SCENE

STORY EVENT

A Story Event is an active change of a universal human value for one or more characters as a result of conflict (one character's desires clash with another's, or an environmental shift changes the value positively or negatively).

A Working Scene contains at least one Story Event. To determine a Scene's Story Event, answer these four Socratic questions:

1. What are the characters literally doing—that is, what are their micro on-the-surface actions?

This is a "meet and greet" scene. Sheppard and the house party at Fernly Park greet each other and gather for dinner.

2. What is the essential tactic of the characters—that is, what above-the-surface macro behaviors are they employing that are linked to a universal human value?

Sheppard checks out the house to set up the murder. Mrs. Ackroyd wants Sheppard to talk to Ackroyd for her.

3. What beyond-the-surface universal human values have changed for one or more characters in the scene? Which one of those value changes is most important and should be included in the Story Grid Spreadsheet?

While Sheppard notes a few suspicious activities before dinner, Mrs. Ackroyd corners him to ask Roger to provide for Flora upon her marriage.
Free (+) to Cornered (-)

4. The Scene Event Synthesis: What Story Event sums up the scene's on-the-surface, above-the-surface, and beyond-the-surface change? We will enter that event in the Story Grid Spreadsheet.

Sheppard introduces the house party at Fernly Park, and Mrs. Ackroyd corners him to request his help in securing support for Flora.

HOW THE SCENE ABIDES BY THE FIVE COMMANDMENTS OF STORYTELLING

Inciting Incident: Sheppard arrives at Fernly Park for dinner.

Progressive Complication: Flora shares news of her engagement to Ralph with Sheppard.

Turning Point Progressive Complication: Active. Mrs. Ackroyd wants Sheppard to intercede on Flora's behalf and make sure Roger intends to give Flora money when she marries Ralph.

Crisis: Best Bad Choice. To acquiesce to Mrs. Ackroyd's request would be really awkward for Sheppard. To decline it would cause her to be insufferable.

Climax: Sheppard is spared from having to answer by the other guests' arrival.

Resolution: Everyone is introduced and sits down to dinner. Roger Ackroyd is silent and sullen throughout dinner.

NOTE

- This is an exposition scene to introduce the suspects. There is no global justice value shift. The purpose is to create suspicion and set the stage for murder.

CHAPTER 4: DINNER AT FERNLY

PART II: SCENE 5 (AFTER DINNER)

2653 words

"Immediately after dinner Ackroyd slipped ... just found Roger Ackroyd murdered."

Summary: Alone in his study, Ackroyd tells Sheppard that Mrs. Ferrars confessed to killing her husband and that she has been blackmailed. A letter from Mrs. Ferrars arrives. Sheppard leaves the study, finds Parker eavesdropping, and tells him that Mr. Ackroyd is not to be disturbed. Sheppard runs into a stranger asking for directions to Fernly Park. As he's going to bed, he gets a call and tells Caroline it was Parker and that Mr. Ackroyd has been found murdered.

ANALYZING THE SCENE

STORY EVENT

A Story Event is an active change of a universal human value for one or more characters as a result of conflict (one character's desires clash with another's, or an environmental shift changes the value positively or negatively).

A Working Scene contains at least one Story Event. To determine a scene's Story Event, answer these four Socratic questions:

1. What are the characters literally doing—that is, what are their micro on-the-surface actions?

Ackroyd and Sheppard speak privately in his office. A letter arrives from beyond the grave. Sheppard claims to receive a call from Parker that Ackroyd has been murdered.

2. What is the essential tactic of the characters—that is, what above-the-surface macro behaviors are they employing that are linked to a universal human value?

When Mrs. Ferrars's letter arrives, Sheppard murders Ackroyd and leaves the study with orders for Ackroyd to be left undisturbed. He returns home and receives a prearranged call announcing Ackroyd's murder, calling him back to Fernly.

3. What beyond-the-surface universal human values have changed for one or more characters in the scene? Which one of those value changes is most important and should be included in the Story Grid Spreadsheet?

The letter's arrival seals Ackroyd's fate.
Danger (-) To Doom (--)

4. The Scene Event Synthesis: What Story Event sums up the scene's on-the-surface, above-the-surface, and beyond-the-surface change? We will enter that event in the Story Grid Spreadsheet.

Sheppard murders Ackroyd after Mrs. Ferrars's letter arrives.

HOW THE SCENE ABIDES BY THE FIVE COMMANDMENTS OF STORYTELLING

Inciting Incident: Causal. Roger Ackroyd tells Sheppard that Mrs. Ferrars confessed to poisoning her husband.

Progressive Complication: Mrs. Ferrars had told Ackroyd that she was being blackmailed but wouldn't reveal the name for twenty-four hours.

Turning Point Progressive Complication: Active. A letter from Mrs. Ferrars arrives detailing the blackmail and presumably including the name of the blackmailer.

Crisis: Best bad choice. Now that Ackroyd has the whole truth in his hands, what are Sheppard's options? Ackroyd cannot be bribed. Sheppard must either turn himself in or silence Ackroyd to protect himself.

Climax: Sheppard murders Ackroyd and burns the letter as he has planned to do.

Resolution: Sheppard returns home and waits to be called back to Fernly.

NOTES

- Convention: *MacGuffin.* This is the tangible want of the villain. Sheppard kills for the letter naming him as the blackmailer.
- Convention: *Clock.* Sheppard races to get everything set up in time.

CHAPTER 5: MURDER
SCENE 6

3497 words

"I got out the car ... Then I hurried downstairs again."

Summary: Within five minutes of the call, Sheppard arrives again at Fernly Park. Parker says he made no call. They bust through the locked study door to find Mr. Ackroyd indeed murdered—stabbed from behind. Parker calls the police while Sheppard examines the body. The inspector arrives. Sheppard, Blunt, Raymond, Flora, and Parker tell him when they last saw Ackroyd. Flora faints when the inspector tells her Ackroyd has been murdered.

ANALYZING THE SCENE

STORY EVENT

A Story Event is an active change of a universal human value for one or more characters as a result of conflict (one character's desires clash with another's, or an environmental shift changes the value positively or negatively).

A Working Scene contains at least one Story Event. To determine a scene's Story Event, answer these four Socratic questions:

1. What are the characters literally doing—that is, what are their micro on-the-surface actions?

Sheppard breaks into Ackroyd's study and finds him murdered. The investigator arrives and begins questioning the household.

2. What is the essential tactic of the characters—that is, what above-the-surface macro behaviors are they employing that are linked to a universal human value?

Sheppard and Parker find Ackroyd's dead body in the study. The police investigate. Flora wants to avoid questions about what she was doing near the study.

3. What beyond-the-surface universal human values have changed for one or more characters in the scene? Which one of those value changes is most important and should be included in the Story Grid Spreadsheet?

We'll track the value for Roger Ackroyd in this scene as this is the obligatory dead body scene.

Life (+) to Murder (--)

4. The Scene Event Synthesis: What Story Event sums up the scene's on-the-surface, above-the-surface, and beyond-the-surface change? We will enter that event in the Story Grid Spreadsheet.

Sheppard and Parker find Ackroyd's dead body in the study, and the police investigate.

HOW THE SCENE ABIDES BY THE FIVE COMMANDMENTS OF STORYTELLING

Inciting Incident: Causal. Sheppard arrives at Fernly to see Mr. Ackroyd.

Progressive Complications: Parker denies making the call. The study door is locked. Ackroyd does not answer.

Turning Point Progressive Complication: Revelatory. Mr. Ackroyd is discovered murdered.

Crisis: Irreconcilable goods choice. To get the time of death right, the inspector asks Flora about her interaction with her uncle at 9:45 p.m. Flora is trapped in a lie. Admitting she didn't talk to him would bring up questions as to why she was in that area in the first place. What harm could lying do?

Climax: Flora makes up an exchange between her and her uncle.

Resolution: Flora faints when told her uncle had been murdered not robbed.

NOTES

- Obligatory moment: *Dead Body*. Though we learn later that Ackroyd was murdered during the last chapter, a Murder Mystery requires an on-page dead body. This scene has several conventions rolled into one. An investigator character is introduced, the police begin following the clues, and Red Herrings pop up all over the place.
- Do you notice how the abundance of details muddies the clarity of the timeline?
- Do you notice we only get the narrator's side of the call? "I'll give you the exact words I heard. 'Is that Sheppard? Parker, the butler at Fernly, speaking. Will you please come at once,

sir. Mr. Ackroyd has been murdered.'" Sheppard reports the words from the caller.

- Revelation: Sheppard can get to Fernly in five minutes by car.
- The core of the scene happens in the beginning. The inspector arrives at Fernly, and the investigation begins. There are revelations in the investigation beat. You could go crazy with the Five Commandments and break down the beat after the inspector arrives.
- Christie frames the inspector's interview of Flora as hunting down a thief, not a murderer. Flora is cornered, though the rest don't know; she was in the study area because she was stealing from her uncle's bedroom (the stairs leading to his room are next to the study) when Parker saw her. If she had known it was murder, she may not have lied.
- Convention: *Red Herrings*. False clues include locked study, letter from Mrs. Ferrars missing, shoe prints outside the window, and a demand for money overheard.
- Convention: *Red Herrings*. Misleading alibis lead to an incorrect timeline. Raymond heard Ackroyd speaking at 9:30 p.m.; Flora said he did not want to be disturbed at 9:45 p.m.
- Convention: *Investigator*. Inspector Davis airs his theory.
- Obligatory Moments: *Following the Clues*

CHAPTER 6: THE TUNISIAN DAGGER

SCENE 7

2373 words

"I met the inspector just ... we went up to bed."

Summary: The inspector and the characters look over the murder weapon, the dagger. Parker is revealed to have eavesdropped on Sheppard's conversation with Ackroyd. He becomes the prime suspect for Inspector Davis. That theory is debated and rejected by the others as too obvious. Anyone (including someone standing outside the open window) could have had access to the dagger in the silver table.

ANALYZING THE SCENE

STORY EVENT

A Story Event is an active change of a universal human value for one or more characters as a result of conflict (one character's desires clash with

another's, or an environmental shift changes the value positively or negatively).

A Working Scene contains at least one Story Event. To determine a scene's Story Event, answer these four Socratic questions:

1. What are the characters literally doing—that is, what are their micro on-the-surface actions?

Inspector Davis confides in Sheppard that he doesn't trust Parker. Sheppard examines the body and the murder weapon.

2. What is the essential tactic of the characters—that is, what above-the-surface macro behaviors are they employing that are linked to a universal human value?

Parker admits overhearing something about blackmail. Blunt and Raymond identify the murder weapon, which was kept in the silver table in the drawing room. Davis not-so-slyly takes Parker's fingerprints to compare with those on the dagger. Davis is eager for a suspect and overconfident in his theory and his notice of the fingerprints.

3. What beyond-the-surface universal human values have changed for one or more characters in the scene? Which one of those value changes is most important and should be included in the Story Grid Spreadsheet?

Anyone could have taken the dagger. Davis is happy to have a suspect.

Let's track the life value for Inspector Davis, the bumbling policeman eager to wrap up the case with the simple solution.

Eager (+) to Overconfident (-)

4. The Scene Event Synthesis: What Story Event sums up the scene's on-the-surface, above-the-surface, and beyond-the-surface change? We will enter that event in the Story Grid Spreadsheet.

Inspector Davis hastily suspects Parker, the butler.

HOW THE SCENE ABIDES BY THE FIVE COMMANDMENTS OF STORYTELLING

Inciting Incident: Causal. Inspector Davis invites Sheppard to a private conversation.

Progressive Complication: The letter from Mrs. Ferrars has disappeared. Parker told Davis about overhearing something about blackmail outside the study.

Turning Point Progressive Complication: Revelatory. The murder weapon was kept in the silver table in the drawing room, which Sheppard heard close before dinner.

Crisis: Irreconcilable goods choice. If Sheppard makes a big deal about this point, he can throw suspicion on Miss Russell. Miss Russell will have to give an account of leaving the drawing room in a hurry.

Climax: Miss Russell stumbles and then says she was in the drawing room to freshen the flowers.

Resolution: Davis still suspects Parker of being the blackmailer and the murderer. Caroline dismisses this theory when Sheppard returns home.

NOTES

- Convention: *Prime suspect*
- Obligatory moment: *Following the Clues*
- The murder has been committed and the investigation begun. We've met most of our suspects.

CHAPTER 7: I LEARN MY NEIGHBOUR'S PROFESSION

SCENE 8

3786 words

"On the following morning I ... night mail leaves for Liverpool."

Summary: Flora asks Sheppard to help coerce Poirot to investigate the crime. She knows Ralph is soon to be named the prime suspect by the new detective on the case, Inspector Raglan. Poirot agrees, with the promise (or threat) to discover the truth. Poirot and Sheppard visit the police station and learn that Ralph is a suspect. They continue to Fernly where Poirot inspects the room as it was the night before. Parker reveals that a grandfather chair was pushed out when they found the body and then pushed back when he came back with the police. The call from "Parker" was actually placed at King's Abbot Station at 10:15 p.m.

ANALYZING THE SCENE

STORY EVENT

A Story Event is an active change of a universal human value for one or more characters as a result of conflict (one character's desires clash with another's, or an environmental shift changes the value positively or negatively).

A Working Scene contains at least one Story Event. To determine a scene's Story Event, answer these four Socratic questions:

1. What are the characters literally doing—that is, what are their micro on-the-surface actions?

Flora enlists Hercule Poirot as investigator to clear Ralph as the prime suspect. The master detective takes on the case and begins investigating.

2. What is the essential tactic of the characters—that is, what above-the-surface macro behaviors are they employing that are linked to a universal human value?

Flora Ackroyd believes Ralph is innocent but understands that he appears guilty. She wants to hire Hercule Poirot, Master Detective, to investigate.

3. What beyond-the-surface universal human values have changed for one or more characters in the scene? Which one of those value changes is most important and should be included in the Story Grid Spreadsheet?

We'll track the value for our protagonist, Poirot, now that he is on the scene. The investigator will move toward Justice.
Bored with Retirement (-) to Employed and Intrigued (+)

4. The Scene Event Synthesis: What Story Event sums up the scene's on-the-surface, above-the-surface, and beyond-the-surface change? We will enter that event in the Story Grid Spreadsheet.

Flora hires Hercule Poirot, Master Detective, to investigate Ackroyd's murder.

HOW THE SCENE ABIDES BY THE FIVE COMMANDMENTS OF STORYTELLING

Inciting Incident: Causal. Flora asks Sheppard to help her convince Poirot to investigate Ackroyd's murder.

Progressive Complication: Poirot's identity is revealed. A new inspector, Raglan, has been assigned. Ralph Paton, Flora's fiancé, is a suspect.

Turning Point Progressive Complication: Active. Flora begs Poirot to investigate.

Crisis: Irreconcilable goods choice. If Poirot takes the case, he will find the truth—whether or not it clears Ralph. The truth is not good for everyone.

Climax: Poirot takes the case.

Resolution: Poirot investigates the scene of the crime. They learn that the call from Parker was placed at King's Abbot Station. (Cliffhanger)

NOTES

- The inciting incident of the middle build is when Flora enlists Hercule Poirot to the case.
- Hercule Poirot is the protagonist and master detective of the story. As the investigator with both a conscious want (solve the murder) and an unconscious need (to serve Truth) based in justice, we consider Poirot's value shift and the global story value when analyzing the turn of the scene.
- Off-stage, Ralph Paton has become the prime suspect. It's an interesting choice to move from on-stage accusation of Parker to off-stage accusation of Ralph.

- "I had hoped that visit of mine would remain unnoticed."
  We learn from Flora that Sheppard went to the Three Boars
  the night before, which he did not tell us. This is the first
  omission by Sheppard that we become aware of. This
  introduces his potential to be unreliable.
- Convention: *Clue*. Sheppard left the chair pushed out,
  thinking Parker would not notice. The boot prints are really
  a *Red Herring* as Sheppard works to implicate Ralph.
- Convention: *Master detective as investigator*
- Obligatory Moment: *Following the Clues*

ACT II: THE MIDDLE BUILD

POIROT'S INVESTIGATION

CHAPTER 8: INSPECTOR RAGLAN IS CONFIDENT

SCENE 9

3037 words

"We looked at each other ... scrap carefully in his pocketbook."

Summary: Poirot continues investigating at Fernly. Raglan is prepared to make a case against Ralph Paton. Poirot and Sheppard explore the grounds without Raglan.

ANALYZING THE SCENE

STORY EVENT

A Story Event is an active change of a universal human value for one or more characters as a result of conflict (one character's desires clash with another's, or an environmental shift changes the value positively or negatively).

A Working Scene contains at least one Story Event. To determine a scene's Story Event, answer these four Socratic questions:

1. What are the characters literally doing—that is, what are their micro on-the-surface actions?

As Poirot continues to inspect the scene of the crime, Raglan airs his theory against Ralph and shares the alibis of the rest of the household. Poirot asks Sheppard about the American stranger. Raymond says a salesman from a dictaphone company came to sell a dictaphone but was turned down. Poirot finds a goose quill and a piece of fabric in the summerhouse.

2. What is the essential tactic of the characters—that is, what above-the-surface macro behaviors are they employing that are linked to a universal human value?

Ralph Paton is Raglan's prime suspect. Sheppard becomes Poirot's sidekick, like Captain Hastings or Sherlock's Watson.

3. What beyond-the-surface universal human values have changed for one or more characters in the scene? Which one of those value changes is most important and should be included in the Story Grid Spreadsheet?

Sheppard needs to be included in the investigation. Poirot needs the Truth; he is unconvinced with Raglan's theory.
We'll track the life value for Raglan in this scene.
Theory (+) to Blind Confidence (- -)

4. The Scene Event Synthesis: What Story Event sums up the scene's on-the-surface, above-the-surface, and beyond-the-surface change? We will enter that event in the Story Grid Spreadsheet.

Inspector Raglan names Ralph Paton as his prime suspect.

HOW THE SCENE ABIDES BY THE FIVE COMMANDMENTS OF STORYTELLING

Inciting Incident: Coincidental. It's revealed that the call came from King's Abbot Station (previous scene).

Progressive Complication: The clues are progressively complicated throughout this scene, which is a convention of the Murder Mystery subgenre.

Turning Point Progressive Complication: Revelatory. Mary Black saw Ralph at Fernly Park at 9:25 p.m.

Crisis: Best Bad Choice. Poirot can interrupt, or he can leave Raglan to his theory.

Climax: Poirot interrupts.

Resolution: Raglan dismisses Poirot's question and continues to investigate. Poirot enlists Sheppard as his Watson.

NOTES

- Theory: "It's all clear enough. It fits in without a flaw." The inspector airs his surest theory, which even the newest Murder Mystery reader knows is not right. It's too easy.
- Poirot has a habit of not finishing his sentences, a useful tool of subtext.
- Convention: *Clues/Red Herrings*. "An opened window, a locked door, a chair that moved itself," shoes found in Ralph's room match the shoe prints outside, torn fabric and a goose quill, Ralph's motive
- Convention: *Watson/Sidekick*. Sheppard becomes Poirot's Watson, assisting and narrating his investigation.
- Obligatory moment: *Following the Clues*

CHAPTER 9: THE GOLDFISH POND
SCENE 10

2567 words

"We walked back to the ... not intend to be communicative."

Summary: Sheppard and Poirot overhear a tense and somewhat flirtatious conversation between Flora and Blunt. After spying for some time, Poirot steps in to introduce himself to Blunt and ask him some questions.

ANALYZING THE SCENE

STORY EVENT

A Story Event is an active change of a universal human value for one or more characters as a result of conflict (one character's desires clash with another's, or an environmental shift changes the value positively or negatively).

A Working Scene contains at least one Story Event. To determine a scene's Story Event, answer these four Socratic questions:

1. What are the characters literally doing—that is, what are their micro on-the-surface actions?

Poirot and Sheppard spy on Flora and Major Blunt discussing Ackroyd's death and Ralph's alleged guilt. Flora reveals a motive. Her inheritance will free her from the family and her unhappy lifestyle. Blunt talks about hunting, with a veiled point that a gun would be his weapon of choice. Poirot questions Blunt and then fishes a gold wedding band out of the pond.

2. What is the essential tactic of the characters—that is, what above-the-surface macro behaviors are they employing that are linked to a universal human value?

Flora reveals a motive for murder and that she clearly has secrets. Sheppard is concerned about eavesdropping. Without her uncle's control, Flora is free to not marry Ralph.

3. What beyond-the-surface universal human values have changed for one or more characters in the scene? Which one of those value changes is most important and should be included in the Story Grid Spreadsheet?

We'll track the value for Flora in this scene as she reveals a motive for murder.
Flora: *Bound (-) to Free (++)*

4. The Scene Event Synthesis: What Story Event sums up the scene's on-the-surface, above-the-surface, and beyond-the-surface change? We will enter that event in the Story Grid Spreadsheet.

Flora is liberated by her uncle's death to marry and live as she pleases.

HOW THE SCENE ABIDES BY THE FIVE COMMANDMENTS OF STORYTELLING

Inciting Incident: Causal: Blunt approaches Flora.

Turning Point Progressive Complication: Revelatory. Flora reveals a potential motive for murder. She inherits enough money to be free of the family.

Crisis: Irreconcilable goods choice. Should Poirot and Sheppard reveal their vantage point? Will they learn more in the shadows or on stage?

Climax: Poirot and Sheppard join Flora and Blunt by the pond.

Resolution: Poirot finds another clue—the gold ring inscribed with *"From R., March 13th."*

NOTE

- Christie has Poirot and Sheppard observe Blunt and Flora to learn some of their true thoughts and motives before moving in on them.

CHAPTER 10: THE PARLOURMAID
SCENE 11

3997 words

"We found Mrs. Ackroyd in ... But very sure indeed."

Summary: Poirot and Sheppard talk with Hammond about Ackroyd's will and Ralph's money troubles. When Hammond asks Mrs. Ackroyd if she has enough cash, Raymond asserts that Ackroyd had withdrawn one hundred pounds the day before, of which we learn that forty pounds are missing. Inspector Raglan and Poirot interview the servants Ursula Bourne, Elsie Dale, and Miss Russell about the missing money. Poirot is interested in Ursula's lack of confirmed alibi and her quitting the day of the murder after a minor conflict with Ackroyd.

ANALYZING THE SCENE

STORY EVENT

43

A Story Event is an active change of a universal human value for one or more characters as a result of conflict (one character's desires clash with another's, or an environmental shift changes the value positively or negatively).

A Working Scene contains at least one Story Event. To determine a scene's Story Event, answer these four Socratic questions:

1. What are the characters literally doing—that is, what are their micro on-the-surface actions?

Poirot discusses Ackroyd's will with Hammond and learns that Ackroyd left almost everything to Ralph. Poirot and Sheppard interview the servants after it's discovered that forty pounds has gone missing.

2. What is the essential tactic of the characters—that is, what above-the-surface macro behaviors are they employing that are linked to a universal human value?

Forty pounds are missing from Ackroyd's bedroom. The servants are interrogated, and Ursula has no alibi and no defense. Mrs. Ackroyd acts nervous and offers a flimsy theory of "accidental death." Poirot asks Sheppard to ask the questions he wants answers to. Mrs. Ackroyd expresses concerns about Miss Russell.

3. What beyond-the-surface universal human values have changed for one or more characters in the scene? Which one of those value changes is most important and should be included in the Story Grid Spreadsheet?

The cast of suspects widens as the servants are called into question. Ursula was able to hide in the background before, but now she is under scrutiny. Let's track the value for the servants, particularly Ursula.

Ignored (+) to Under Scrutiny (-)

4. The Scene Event Synthesis: What Story Event sums up the scene's

on-the-surface, above-the-surface, and beyond-the-surface change? We will enter that event in the Story Grid Spreadsheet.

Ursula Bourne is suspected and disgraced.

HOW THE SCENE ABIDES BY THE FIVE COMMANDMENTS OF STORYTELLING

Inciting Incident: Causal. Mr. Hammond, the family lawyer, lays out the terms of the will.

Progressive Complication: Ralph, who was always hard-pressed for money, will inherit the whole estate. Colonel Blunt inherited a legacy recently.

Turning Point Progressive Complication: Revelatory. Forty pounds are missing from Ackroyd's locked bedroom.

Crisis: Best bad choice. Will Ursula tell the truth about her dismissal? She becomes a suspect if she doesn't; she may incriminate Ralph more if she does.
Off the page: Irreconcilable goods choice. When Poirot asks Sheppard about Ursula, does he reveal what he knows about Ursula and Ralph, or does he keep his mouth shut and condemn them both further?

Climax: Ursula stays quiet on the matter (as does Sheppard).

Resolution: Poirot will continue to seek to exonerate Ralph.

NOTES

- "We ate lunch." There is no lunch scene. Christie opted not to include it. She could have introduced the house maid and the parlor maid during lunch, in a more servile capacity. But instead, she used a twist—*money has gone missing from the dead man's locked bedroom*—to bring these characters onto the set.

- Mrs. Ackroyd provides comic relief in her "sensitive nerves" and her ridiculous theory of accidental death to avoid unpleasantness.
- "You and I, M. le docteur, we investigate this affair side by side." Convenient location for the criminal to remain intimate to the investigation (and for the detective to get all his answers).
- Conventions: *Clue.* The missing forty pounds points to another crime in the house on the night of the murder.

CHAPTER 11: POIROT PAYS A CALL
SCENE 12

2097 words

"I was slightly nervous when ... have peace in the home."

Summary: Against his wishes, Sheppard interviews Mrs. Folliott alone to get a reference for Ursula. He leaves with no information. When he returns home, Caroline announces that Poirot came to visit and asked a lot of questions. He had asked about Sheppard's patients the day of the murder, with a focus on Miss Russell. Sheppard wonders why Poirot came to call while he was out.

ANALYZING THE SCENE

STORY EVENT

A Story Event is an active change of a universal human value for one or more characters as a result of conflict (one character's desires clash with

another's, or an environmental shift changes the value positively or negatively).

A Working Scene contains at least one Story Event. To determine a scene's Story Event, answer these four Socratic questions:

1. What are the characters literally doing—that is, what are their micro on-the-surface actions?

Sheppard talks to Mrs. Folliott while Poirot talks with Caroline.

2. What is the essential tactic of the characters—that is, what above-the-surface macro behaviors are they employing that are linked to a universal human value?

Sheppard and Poirot have two separate interviews. Poirot hopes to get information on Sheppard from Caroline. Sheppard does Poirot's bidding and is rather annoyed.

3. What beyond-the-surface universal human values have changed for one or more characters in the scene? Which one of those value changes is most important and should be included in the Story Grid Spreadsheet?

Sheppard does not feel like Watson. Poirot seems to have intentionally operated without him. Let's track Sheppard's life value.
Involved (+) to Left Out (-)

4. The Scene Event Synthesis: What Story Event sums up the scene's on-the-surface, above-the-surface, and beyond-the-surface change? We will enter that event in the Story Grid Spreadsheet.

Poirot sends Sheppard on a wild goose chase.

HOW THE SCENE ABIDES BY THE FIVE COMMANDMENTS OF STORYTELLING

Inciting Incident: Causal. Sheppard calls on Mrs. Folliott to get a reference for Ursula on Poirot's behalf.

Turning Point Progressive Complication: Revelatory. Poirot called on Caroline while Sheppard was out.

Crisis: Irreconcilable goods choice. Caroline loves being the holder of information. If she gives it up, the game is over, but she looks important. The longer she drags it out, the more she will irritate her brother.

Climax: Caroline reveals that she told Poirot all about Sheppard's patients on the day of the murder. She and Poirot think there's "something fishy" about Miss Russell.

Resolution: Sheppard ponders the importance of Miss Russell's visit. He goes down to dinner to have peace in the house.

NOTES

- Poirot sends Sheppard on a wild goose chase to get his sister alone. Sheppard is, after all, a suspect (though he is made to feel like Poirot's sidekick).
- This is a great way to outmaneuver the limitation of a first-person narrator. Sheppard receives the information secondhand, and his sister recounts off-stage events. Christie does this to keep the reader and the narrator in the dark.

CHAPTER 12: ROUND THE TABLE

SCENE 13

2470 words

"A joint inquest was held ... he said, and went out."

Summary: The scene opens with a discussion between Poirot, Sheppard, and Raglan about how bleak the case against Ralph looks and how confusing the clues are, such as the telephone call and the odd fingerprints on the dagger. After the inquest and a conversation with Raglan, Poirot assembles the household.

ANALYZING THE SCENE

STORY EVENT

A Story Event is an active change of a universal human value for one or more characters as a result of conflict (one character's desires clash with

another's, or an environmental shift changes the value positively or negatively).

A Working Scene contains at least one Story Event. To determine a scene's Story Event, answer these four Socratic questions:

1. What are the characters literally doing—that is, what are their micro on-the-surface actions?

Poirot beseeches Flora to reach out to Ralph. Flora insists she doesn't know how and plans to announce her engagement to him. Poirot dissuades her. He demands to hear everyone's secrets, to which no one responds.

2. What is the essential tactic of the characters—that is, what above-the-surface macro behaviors are they employing that are linked to a universal human value?

Poirot threatens the group; they can bare their secrets or be exposed. They refuse to speak up. Mrs. Ackroyd wants Flora to break off the engagement. Poirot wants to know where Ralph is.

3. What beyond-the-surface universal human values have changed for one or more characters in the scene? Which one of those value changes is most important and should be included in the Story Grid Spreadsheet?

Let's take the life value for Poirot as he makes a move toward knowing.

Poirot threatens the group as a whole. He moves from being an ally to most to being a threat to all.

Ally (+) to Threat (-)

4. The Scene Event Synthesis: What Story Event sums up the scene's on-the-surface, above-the-surface, and beyond-the-surface change? We will enter that event in the Story Grid Spreadsheet.

Poirot threatens the group to bare their secrets or be exposed.

HOW THE SCENE ABIDES BY THE FIVE COMMANDMENTS OF STORYTELLING

Inciting Incident: The police hold an inquest.

Progressive Complication: Poirot suggests the fingerprints on the dagger are Ackroyd's own. He gathers everyone around a table.

Turning Point Progressive Complication: Active. Poirot threatens the members of the household, in a sense. "I mean to know, in spite of you all. Tell me the truth—the whole truth."

Crisis: Best bad choice. Will everyone—or anyone—bare their secrets, or will Poirot have to investigate and drag them out?

Climax: No one speaks up.

Resolution: They have missed their opportunity. Poirot will set to work uncovering their secrets, to their peril.

NOTES

- The inquest happens off stage, without report. There are two beats "on stage" in this scene. First, Raglan, Poirot, and Sheppard discuss the fingerprints and the telephone call and debate their significance. This is a positive result for Sheppard in that he is at Poirot's side again. The next beat is a "family reunion," an archetypal meeting scene. Sheppard is not privy to Poirot's true motives for this "séance," so he's not fully involved.
- The core of the scene is the shift from Poirot's role as an ally to a potential threat as he seeks out justice. The next sequence of scenes involves the characters (suspects) coming forward and revealing their secrets. Poirot's challenge is the

turning point of the story before the *global crisis* (Will Poirot see the through the Red Herrings and find the murderer?) so let's take the value shift at this point.

- Poirot foreshadows the Smoking Gun Clue—the telephone call. "I believe that when we find the explanation for that telephone call, we shall know the explanation for the murder."
- Convention: *Clock.* Poirot institutes a clock for the suspects. Either they confess their secrets now, or he will find them out and expose them.

CHAPTER 13: THE GOOSE QUILL
SCENE 14

1927 words

"That evening, at Poirot's request ... all, Ralph Paton is innocent."

Summary: Poirot invites Sheppard for dinner and tells him he has verified the statements that Sheppard left Fernly Park at 9 p.m. and that the mysterious American stranger did exist. Sheppard lays out his own theory and his take on the clues. He suspects the American stranger, perhaps in conjunction with Parker as the blackmailer. Poirot is dissatisfied with this theory because of gaps in the evidence, including the pushed-out chair. Poirot counts three motives against Ralph Paton, which he thinks are too coincidental. He believes this actually proves Ralph is innocent.

ANALYZING THE SCENE

STORY EVENT

A Story Event is an active change of a universal human value for one or more characters as a result of conflict (one character's desires clash with another's, or an environmental shift changes the value positively or negatively).

A Working Scene contains at least one Story Event. To determine a scene's Story Event, answer these four Socratic questions:

1. What are the characters literally doing—that is, what are their micro on-the-surface actions?

Poirot and Sheppard discuss their theories and methods.

2. What is the essential tactic of the characters—that is, what above-the-surface macro behaviors are they employing that are linked to a universal human value?

Sheppard attempts to divert suspicion with the American stranger. Poirot does not name his suspect but believes Ralph looks too guilty to actually be guilty.

3. What beyond-the-surface universal human values have changed for one or more characters in the scene? Which one of those value changes is most important and should be included in the Story Grid Spreadsheet?

Let's track the value for Ralph in this scene as Poirot believes the preponderance of motives clears him.
Presumed Guilty (-) to Believed Innocent (+)

4. The Scene Event Synthesis: What Story Event sums up the scene's on-the-surface, above-the-surface, and beyond-the-surface change? We will enter that event in the Story Grid Spreadsheet.

Poirot thwarts Sheppard's attempts to incriminate Ralph.

HOW THE SCENE ABIDES BY THE FIVE COMMANDMENTS OF STORYTELLING

Inciting Incident: Causal. Sheppard is invited to dinner at Poirot's home.

Progressive Complication: The goose quill that Poirot found at Fernly Park suggests a heroin-user was in the summerhouse that night.

Turning Point Progressive Complication: Active. Poirot asks Sheppard's theory.

Crisis: Irreconcilable goods choice. Who should Sheppard accuse to throw suspicion off himself?

Climax: Sheppard accuses the American stranger.

Resolution: Poirot decides the case against Ralph is too conveniently tidy.

NOTES

- A rare two-person scene signals to the reader that Sheppard and Poirot are a team.
- Poirot reveals bits and pieces of his theories relating to the goose quill and Ralph's innocence, leaving questions in the reader's and the narrator's minds. This is an example of the form of narrative drive we call *mystery*. Poirot knows more than the reader.

CHAPTER 14: MRS. ACKROYD
SCENE 15

3179 words

"After the evening talk, I ... to do with the case."

Summary: Poirot's threat has landed with Mrs. Ackroyd, and she tediously explains her own secrets from the night of the murder to Sheppard so he will tell Poirot for her. She was the one who left the silver table open. In the next beat, Sheppard confronts Ursula for having lied about Ackroyd calling for her to dismiss her. Sheppard goes home. Caroline smugly relates her involvement in the investigation, as she has helped Poirot figure out that Ralph's boots are black.

ANALYZING THE SCENE

STORY EVENT

A Story Event is an active change of a universal human value for one or more characters as a result of conflict (one character's desires clash with another's, or an environmental shift changes the value positively or negatively).

A Working Scene contains at least one Story Event. To determine a scene's Story Event, answer these four Socratic questions:

1. What are the characters literally doing—that is, what are their micro on-the-surface actions?

Mrs. Ackroyd unburdens herself to Sheppard. Sheppard confronts Ursula, who is caught in a lie. Poirot commissions Caroline to find out about Ralph's boots.

2. What is the essential tactic of the characters—that is, what above-the-surface macro behaviors are they employing that are linked to a universal human value?

Mrs. Ackroyd confesses her secrets to Sheppard, who reads between the lines. Sheppard and Ursula seek information from each other, to no avail. Caroline reports on the color of Ralph's boots. Ursula wants to know where Ralph is and if he's innocent.

3. What beyond-the-surface universal human values have changed for one or more characters in the scene? Which one of those value changes is most important and should be included in the Story Grid Spreadsheet?

We'll track the life value for Mrs. Ackroyd. The case gets a little light from her confessions, only to be muddied again by Ursula's behavior and then Poirot's focus on the trivial matter of the color of the boots.
Guilty (-) to Unburdened (+)

4. The Scene Event Synthesis: What Story Event sums up the scene's on-the-surface, above-the-surface, and beyond-the-surface change? We will enter that event in the Story Grid Spreadsheet.

Mrs. Ackroyd confesses her money troubles.

HOW THE SCENE ABIDES BY THE FIVE COMMANDMENTS OF STORYTELLING

Inciting Incident: Causal. Mrs. Ackroyd sends for Sheppard.

Progressive Complication: Mrs. Ackroyd acts ill. She unburdens herself by telling her secrets. She was in money trouble after getting involved in a scam. Mrs. Ackroyd reveals she was in Ackroyd's study reading his will when Ursula came in and caught her.

Turning Point Progressive Complication: Active. Sheppard confronts Mrs. Ackroyd for leaving the silver table lid open on the night of the murder.

Crisis: Irreconcilable goods choice. Will Sheppard tell Poirot for her, or make her do the work herself?

Climax: Sheppard agrees to tell Poirot on Mrs. Ackroyd's behalf.

Resolution: Sheppard finally gets away from Mrs. Ackroyd.

NOTES

- Interesting commentary from Sheppard: "[Until now], I played Watson to his Sherlock. But after Monday our ways diverged." Sheppard divides the story narration into two parts—as Poirot's confidant, and on the outside.
- In one beat at the end of the chapter, Caroline, commissioned by Poirot, discovers Ralph's boots are black. Sheppard cannot figure out the importance of the clue. It doesn't amount to a shift in the global value, but the Five Commandments of the beat are present.

CHAPTER 15: GEOFFREY RAYMOND

SCENE 16

2548 words

"I was to have a ... us leave it at that."

Summary: Caroline sends Sheppard next door to Poirot. Poirot and Sheppard discuss Mrs. Ackroyd's true movements on the night of the murder. Raymond visits and confesses his secret. When he leaves, Poirot and Sheppard briefly discuss the possibility that blackmail might *not* be the motive for the murder. They go to Fernly to "reconstruct the crime" and to test Parker and Flora. Poirot and Sheppard then walk back to the village, where Poirot says cryptically he has learned "something."

ANALYZING THE SCENE

STORY EVENT

A Story Event is an active change of a universal human value for one or more characters as a result of conflict (one character's desires clash with another's, or an environmental shift changes the value positively or negatively).

A Working Scene contains at least one Story Event. To determine a scene's Story Event, answer these four Socratic questions:

1. What are the characters literally doing—that is, what are their micro on-the-surface actions?

Sheppard visits Poirot. Raymond confesses his secret to Poirot. Poirot and Sheppard go to Fernly to conduct an experiment with Flora and Parker.

2. What is the essential tactic of the characters—that is, what above-the-surface macro behaviors are they employing that are linked to a universal human value?

Raymond reveals a motive for murder—debt. Poirot tests Flora's and Parker's truthfulness.

3. What beyond-the-surface universal human values have changed for one or more characters in the scene? Which one of those value changes is most important and should be included in the Story Grid Spreadsheet?

Let's track the value for Poirot in this scene. Poirot puts some new information and a new theory to the test.

Hypothesis (+) to Experiment (++)

4. The Scene Event Synthesis: What Story Event sums up the scene's on-the-surface, above-the-surface, and beyond-the-surface change? We will enter that event in the Story Grid Spreadsheet.

Raymond admits his debt. Poirot tests Flora and Parker.

HOW THE SCENE ABIDES BY THE FIVE COMMANDMENTS OF STORYTELLING

Inciting Incident: Causal. Geoffrey Raymond calls on Poirot.

Progressive Complication: Raymond's legacy from Ackroyd covers his debts (motive), but he has an alibi. Sheppard suggests the blackmailer may not be the murderer.

Turning Point Progressive Complication: Active. Poirot tests Parker and Flora.

Crisis: Irreconcilable goods choice. Poirot wonders if either Parker or Flora is telling the truth about their interaction outside Ackroyd's study that night.

Climax: Parker corrects Flora's exact words.

Resolution: Poirot has learned something from his experiment but doesn't reveal it.

NOTES

- Notice Raymond's frankness when he admits his secret debt, in contrast to the tedious self-protective narrative of Mrs. Ackroyd in the previous chapter. This is how Christie builds her characters rather than listing characteristics.
- A pattern has emerged in the meat of the middle build. Christie strings together beats and scenes to create *sequences of doubt and clarity*. When clarity arises, such as the forthright telling of a secret or the revelation of an alibi, she quickly muddies the waters by tacking on a beat or scene that further mystifies the reader. The two events in this chapter end positively for the *justice* value, as the primary investigator (Poirot) is gaining more insight into the crime,

but the reader is in the dark (and the narrator's *safety* value is trending down).
- The location changes four times in this chapter, and there are seven different blocks of dialogue. I've evaluated the value shift as it pertains to *justice* across the whole chapter.
- Scene types present: *Having tea/coffee, re-creation of the crime, walk and talk.*

CHAPTER 16: AN EVENING AT MAH JONG
SCENE 17

2698 words

"That night we had a … took it from her meekly."

Summary: Four people play a game and discuss the case, including their own theories and overheard information. Suspicions about Flora, Ursula, and Miss Russell are mentioned. Sheppard recklessly shares information about the gold wedding band ("From R.") as he wins Mah Jong with his original hand, known as the "Perfect Winning."

ANALYZING THE SCENE

STORY EVENT

A Story Event is an active change of a universal human value for one or more characters as a result of conflict (one character's desires clash with

another's, or an environmental shift changes the value positively or negatively).

A Working Scene contains at least one Story Event. To determine a scene's Story Event, answer these four Socratic questions:

1. What are the characters literally doing—that is, what are their micro on-the-surface actions?

Sheppard, Caroline, Miss Gannett, and Colonel Carter play a game of Mah Jong.

2. What is the essential tactic of the characters—that is, what above-the-surface macro behaviors are they employing that are linked to a universal human value?

In the excitement of the game, Sheppard reveals a bit of information about the wedding ring and fuels the gossip.

3. What beyond-the-surface universal human values have changed for one or more characters in the scene? Which one of those value changes is most important and should be included in the Story Grid Spreadsheet?

Let's track the value for Sheppard in this scene.
Losing (-) to Triumphant (+)

4. The Scene Event Synthesis: What Story Event sums up the scene's on-the-surface, above-the-surface, and beyond-the-surface change? We will enter that event in the Story Grid Spreadsheet.

Sheppard wins Mah Jong and spills information about the wedding ring.

HOW THE SCENE ABIDES BY THE FIVE COMMANDMENTS OF STORYTELLING

Inciting Incident: Causal. Colonel Carter comments about the strange case of Ackroyd's murder.

Progressive Complication: Flora was seen with someone about the village. The game ramps up as Miss Gannett wins with poor hands three times in a row.

Turning Point Progressive Complication: Active. Sheppard gets the "Perfect Winning" hand in Mah Jong.

Crisis: Best bad choice. If Sheppard joins in the gossip, he may release too much information. If he stays silent, he'll have to suffer being goaded by Caroline.

Climax: Sheppard tells the others about the wedding ring "From R."

Resolution: The three other players toss around theories of who the married couple could be.

NOTES

- There's definitely some "shoe leather" in this scene. The reader has to wade through the game play to get the information they need. However, the *playing a game* scene type provides progressive complications. It's a way to share information and switch up the *meeting, having coffee,* and *walk and talk* scenes. Because the competition in the game ramps up as it goes along, the tension rises, the stakes get higher, and the intoxication of the Perfect Winning pushes the very careful Sheppard to become overconfident in his triumph. Normally polite, he can't miss an opportunity to mock Carter with a comment ("As we say in the Shanghai Club") and he also uncharacteristically flings out a tidbit of information to prove his mastery of the case.
- This is a great example of character development through

action, not through the description of characteristics. Sheppard's "Perfect Winning" hand is symbolic of the "Perfect Crime." He has gotten too confident.

CHAPTER 17: PARKER

SCENE 18

3644 words

"It occurred to me the ... at once and identify him."

Summary: The joint funeral of Mrs. Ferrars and Ackroyd takes place off stage. Afterward, Poirot invites Sheppard on a couple of fact-finding missions. Sheppard is summoned to Liverpool to identify Charles Kent as the mysterious stranger.

ANALYZING THE SCENE

STORY EVENT

A Story Event is an active change of a universal human value for one or more characters as a result of conflict (one character's desires clash with another's, or an environmental shift changes the value positively or negatively).

A Working Scene contains at least one Story Event. To determine a scene's Story Event, answer these four Socratic questions:

1. What are the characters literally doing—that is, what are their micro on-the-surface actions?

Poirot interviews Parker and Hammond while Sheppard observes. Caroline, Sheppard, and Poirot have lunch and discuss their theories. Poirot accuses Parker of blackmail.

2. What is the essential tactic of the characters—that is, what above-the-surface macro behaviors are they employing that are linked to a universal human value?

Poirot takes Sheppard on some fact-finding missions that help him form a theory of the murderer. Caroline rejects Poirot's theory that someone in the house that night killed Ackroyd. Poirot describes the murderer without accusing anyone.

3. What beyond-the-surface universal human values have changed for one or more characters in the scene? Which one of those value changes is most important and should be included in the Story Grid Spreadsheet?

Let's track the value for Poirot. He learns some information on his fact-finding trips that helps him form the silhouette of the murderer.
Red Herrings (-) to Theory (+)

4. The Scene Event Synthesis: What Story Event sums up the scene's on-the-surface, above-the-surface, and beyond-the-surface change? We will enter that event in the Story Grid Spreadsheet.

Poirot takes Sheppard on some fact-finding missions that help him form a theory of the murderer.

HOW THE SCENE ABIDES BY THE FIVE COMMANDMENTS OF STORYTELLING

Inciting Incident: Causal. Parker comes to the Larches under Poirot's invitation.

Progressive Complication: Poirot accuses Parker of blackmailing his last master. Hammond reveals that Mrs. Ferrars paid out twenty thousand pounds suspiciously.

Turning Point Progressive Complication: Active. Caroline asks Poirot who he thinks committed the murder.

Crisis: Best bad choice. How could Poirot present his theory without putting Sheppard on guard?

Climax: Poirot lays out a picture of the murderer without naming any names. The image could apply to several people, including Ralph, Parker, Blunt, and Sheppard.

Resolution: The police call to have Sheppard identify Charles Kent as the mysterious stranger.

NOTES

- Convention: *Red Herring*. Hector Blunt received a legacy of about twenty thousand pounds (the exact amount Mrs. Ferrars paid out). Was it blackmail, or was it a legitimate legacy?
- Convention: *Red Herring*. Parker blackmailed his last employer.

CHAPTER 18: CHARLES KENT

SCENE 19

1728 words

"Half an hour later saw ... still have my little idea."

Summary: Poirot, Sheppard, and Raglan interview Kent, who is being held by police based on Sheppard's description of the mysterious stranger. Sheppard explains that Poirot had the whole case figured out at this point while he continues to doubt him. Sheppard identifies Kent as the man who asked for directions to Fernly Park on the night of the murder. Kent won't share the reason he was at Fernly that night, since he believes his alibi is solid for the time of murder, 9:45–10 p.m.

ANALYZING THE SCENE

STORY EVENT

A Story Event is an active change of a universal human value for one or more characters as a result of conflict (one character's desires clash with another's, or an environmental shift changes the value positively or negatively).

A Working Scene contains at least one Story Event. To determine a scene's Story Event, answer these four Socratic questions:

1. What are the characters literally doing—that is, what are their micro on-the-surface actions?

Raglan, Poirot, and Sheppard interview a person of interest.

2. What is the essential tactic of the characters—that is, what above-the-surface macro behaviors are they employing that are linked to a universal human value?

Sheppard identifies Kent as the man at Fernly on the night of the murder. Poirot deduces much of the case from the interview. Poirot realizes Kent is Miss Russell's son and a heroin addict.

3. What beyond-the-surface universal human values have changed for one or more characters in the scene? Which one of those value changes is most important and should be included in the Story Grid Spreadsheet?

Let's track the value for Poirot in this scene. Another clue has fallen into place.
Theory (+) to Knowing (++)

4. The Scene Event Synthesis: What Story Event sums up the scene's on-the-surface, above-the-surface, and beyond-the-surface change? We will enter that event in the Story Grid Spreadsheet.

Charles Kent is the mysterious stranger at Fernly Park.

HOW THE SCENE ABIDES BY THE FIVE COMMANDMENTS OF STORYTELLING

Inciting Incident: Causal. Poirot, Sheppard, and Raglan meet Kent in Liverpool.

Progressive Complication: Sheppard recognizes Kent's voice and identifies him as the mysterious stranger.

Turning Point Progressive Complication: Revelatory. The goose quill Poirot found in the summerhouse belonged to Kent.

Crisis: Irreconcilable goods choice. If Kent admits why he was at Fernly late that night, he will incriminate Miss Russell. If he remains silent, he will irritate the police and continue to confuse the case.

Climax: Kent refuses to answer as he believes his alibi is airtight.

Resolution: Poirot knows why Kent was at the house that night "because he was born in Kent."

NOTES

- Convention: *Red Herring*. The fingerprints on the dagger were Ackroyd's.
- Poirot realizes two things from the interview: why Kent was at Fernly that night (to see his mother, Miss Russell); and that the time of death must have been earlier than 9:45 p.m.
- As a master detective, Poirot shows he is superior to the police. Raglan shows his incompetence by claiming Poirot's clue for his own (Ackroyd's fingerprints on the dagger) and by declaring the "whole thing a muddle."
- Convention: *Red Herrings*. Red Herrings arise in the form of *motives*, *alibis*, and *secrets* among other forms. Motive—Does Kent have a motive? Why is Paton staying away? Alibi—

Kent, mysterious stranger, has an alibi, which calls the time of death into question. Secrets—Kent has a secret.

- The mysterious stranger does exist! The reader has doubted his existence, or assumed he is someone associated with the house. The revelation of his identity is shocking and confusing, even while it shines more light on the case for Poirot.

CHAPTER 19: FLORA ACKROYD

SCENE 20

2776 words

"As I was returning from ... kind—the fool in love."

Summary: Kent's alibi checks out. Poirot proposes that the time of death has not been verified. Raglan, Poirot, and Sheppard confront Flora at Fernly Park. She admits she stole the forty pounds, that she is weak (like Ralph), and that she never saw her uncle after dinner the night he was killed. She made up the story to explain her presence near his bedroom and study.

ANALYZING THE SCENE

STORY EVENT

A Story Event is an active change of a universal human value for one or more characters as a result of conflict (one character's desires clash with

75

another's, or an environmental shift changes the value positively or negatively).

A Working Scene contains at least one Story Event. To determine a scene's Story Event, answer these four Socratic questions:

1. What are the characters literally doing—that is, what are their micro on-the-surface actions?

Raglan, Sheppard, and Poirot go to Fernly Park. Poirot confronts Flora, and she confesses. Poirot encourages Blunt to pursue Flora.

2. What is the essential tactic of the characters—that is, what above-the-surface macro behaviors are they employing that are linked to a universal human value?

Poirot questions the veracity of Flora's statement about talking with Ackroyd before he was murdered, which the police have taken for granted. Flora confesses that she lied. She never saw her uncle, and his assumed time of death is thrown off. Blunt claims Ackroyd gave him the money as proof of love for Flora.

3. What beyond-the-surface universal human values have changed for one or more characters in the scene? Which one of those value changes is most important and should be included in the Story Grid Spreadsheet?

At the turning point, we realize the time of death has not been proven, which renders the alibis for 9:45 p.m. useless. This confuses the police and worries Sheppard (who has been conveniently kept safe by Flora's claim), but Poirot views it as positive. Poirot is on the hunt for justice, not for a wrapped-up case. Let's track the value for Poirot, as the global story is a search for justice.

Falsehood Masquerading as Truth (--) to Truth (+)

4. The Scene Event Synthesis: What Story Event sums up the scene's

on-the-surface, above-the-surface, and beyond-the-surface change? We will enter that event in the Story Grid Spreadsheet.

Flora's admission disrupts the whole case.

HOW THE SCENE ABIDES BY THE FIVE COMMANDMENTS OF STORYTELLING

Inciting Incident: Coincidental. Raglan tells Sheppard and Poirot that Kent's alibi for 9:45 p.m. checks out.

Turning Point Progressive Complication: Revelatory. Poirot's experiment with Flora and Parker proved that Parker saw Flora *outside* the study with her hand on the door, not emerging from the study. We only have her word that she saw Roger Ackroyd at 9:45 p.m.

Crisis: Best bad choice. If Flora cops to lying about seeing her uncle at 9:45 that night, she will lose face in front of her family, friends, and the man she secretly loves, Colonel Blunt. However, she will be free of the guilt she's been carrying all along. If she lies, she will continue to be a roadblock in the quest for justice (as well as a hinderer in proving Ralph's innocence) and she will have to continue carrying the guilt.

Climax: Flora confesses.

Resolution: Blunt tries to take the blame. He still loves Flora. Poirot nudges Flora and Blunt together.

NOTES

- Now, where are we with the case? The time of death is false. The mysterious stranger is real. The case is disrupted. The police must start over. This is a convention of Christie's Murder Mysteries. Just when the case is coming together, a curveball baffles everyone. Except for Poirot. It actually helps Poirot iron out what he saw as discrepancies that the other characters accepted as conveniently fitting into their theories.

- Convention: *Red Herring*. Raglan: "The [barmaid] mentions that he had a lot of money on him—she saw him take a handful of notes out of his pocket. Rather surprised her, it did, seeing the class of fellow he was, *with a pair of boots clean dropping off him*. That's where that forty pounds went right enough." (Emphasis added.) Ralph's boots are a Red Herring that Christie continues to harp on. She throws some oversized boots on Kent to make him a suspect.
- Convention: *Red Herring*. Poirot allegedly has a mentally ill nephew. This serves as Poirot's excuse to get into the hospital where Ralph has been stowed away.
- Did Parker see Flora come *out* of her uncle's study or just put her hand on the door? Is Flora's testimony of having seen her uncle alive valid? If not, the whole case is changed. *Time of death is potentially earlier.*
- Blunt loves Flora and is willing to perjure himself to protect her. Flora cares for Blunt and wants him to know who she truly is. Theirs is a complete Courtship Love Story subplot that follows all the obligatory scenes and conventions, though it is subordinate to the overall plot.

CHAPTER 20: MISS RUSSELL
SCENE 21

2967 words

"Inspector Raglan had received a ... much which escaped Hercule Poirot."

SCENE SUMMARY

Poirot visits Sheppard in his tinkering room. Poirot has planted a story in the newspaper to draw out Ralph. Poirot and Sheppard have a meeting with Miss Russell to get her to reveal her secret. Miss Russell is Kent's mother. Kent found out and came to ask for money. Miss Russell is Kent's alibi between when Sheppard saw him and when he was seen at the bar. He seems to be innocent. She also makes Kent *her* alibi in the process.

ANALYZING THE SCENE

STORY EVENT

A Story Event is an active change of a universal human value for one or more characters as a result of conflict (one character's desires clash with another's, or an environmental shift changes the value positively or negatively).

A Working Scene contains at least one Story Event. To determine a scene's Story Event, answer these four Socratic questions:

1. What are the characters literally doing—that is, what are their micro on-the-surface actions?

Poirot and Sheppard interview Miss Russell.

2. What is the essential tactic of the characters—that is, what above-the-surface macro behaviors are they employing that are linked to a universal human value?

Poirot draws out Miss Russell's secret *and* gives Kent an alibi up to 9:25 p.m. Neither Miss Russell nor Kent are truly absolved yet.

3. What beyond-the-surface universal human values have changed for one or more characters in the scene? Which one of those value changes is most important and should be included in the Story Grid Spreadsheet?

Let's track the value for Miss Russell, one of our suspects. Poirot shakes up her ironclad composure by telling her that her son is in danger of conviction.

Imperviousness (+) to Desperation (--)

4. The Scene Event Synthesis: What Story Event sums up the scene's on-the-surface, above-the-surface, and beyond-the-surface change? We will enter that event in the Story Grid Spreadsheet.

Miss Russell's secret and Kent's alibi are revealed but not solidified.

HOW THE SCENE ABIDES BY THE FIVE COMMANDMENTS OF STORYTELLING

Inciting Incident: Causal: Miss Russell arrives at Sheppard's surgery, invited by Poirot.

Progressive Complication: Poirot has planted a false report about Paton in the newspaper.

Turning Point Progressive Complication: Active. Poirot tells Miss Russell that Kent has been arrested for murder. His alibi for 9:45 p.m. is worthless.

Crisis: Best bad choice. Does Miss Russell reveal her shameful secret or let Kent be accused?

Climax: Miss Russell admits that Kent is her illegitimate, drug-addicted son. He came to Fernly to ask her for money.

Resolution: Poirot promises to keep Miss Russell's secret—for now. He departs without eating lunch with Sheppard and Caroline.

NOTES

- In this scene we are introduced to Sheppard's workroom and to his hobby of tinkering.
- Poirot tells Sheppard he could tell the doctor was not surprised by Flora's admission. (Sheppard comes up with an explanation. He had always believed she was holding something back.)
- Breadcrumb: Sheppard's love of machinery and handiness with tinkering forms a quick beat between interview beats.
- The alibis are worthless. "Got to start again."
- Miss Russell provides Kent an alibi and uses him as hers (in confidence of Poirot and Sheppard). Note that these alibis are

not proven, and they are not fully absolved yet. Kent could still be the person talking to Ackroyd at 9:30 p.m. Plus, we know that Poirot will not just take one person's word for it.

- Convention: *Clue.* "Dang that telephone call! We always come up against it."
- Raglan, the incompetent policeman, instantly draws up a new theory when his previous one is shattered. Paton made the call once finding Ackroyd dead to protect himself.
- Poirot conducts a couple of experiments to draw people out: 1) In Sheppard's name, he invites Miss Russell to the doctor's home for an interview. 2) He places a deceitful newspaper ad to draw out Paton.
- Poirot shares his theory: He connected Miss Russell with Kent (mysterious stranger) based on the goose quill (vehicle for heroin) and her questions to Sheppard about drugs the day of the murder.
- Convention: *Red Herring.* Charles Kent is Miss Russell's son.

ACT III: THE ENDING PAYOFF

POIROT RESTORES JUSTICE

CHAPTER 21: THE PARAGRAPH IN THE PAPER

SCENE 22

2059 words

"Caroline, of course had not ... Ursula Paton? Mrs. Ralph Paton."

Summary: The piece in the paper on Ralph's arrest in Liverpool comes out. Caroline is shocked when she reads it and shares her own theories. Poirot will not reveal who his mysterious guest is, despite Caroline's badgering. Poirot commissions Sheppard to gather the entire Fernly Park household at the Larches that night at 9 p.m. Ursula Bourne Paton takes the bait in the paper and comes to see Poirot.

ANALYZING THE SCENE

STORY EVENT

A Story Event is an active change of a universal human value for one or more characters as a result of conflict (one character's desires clash with

another's, or an environmental shift changes the value positively or negatively).

A Working Scene contains at least one Story Event. To determine a scene's Story Event, answer these four Socratic questions:

1. What are the characters literally doing—that is, what are their micro on-the-surface actions?

Poirot commissions Sheppard to invite the household of Fernly Park to the Larches for a summation. Ursula Bourne has seen the story that claims Ralph has been arrested.

2. What is the essential tactic of the characters—that is, what above-the-surface macro behaviors are they employing that are linked to a universal human value?

Poirot gives Sheppard the task of assembling the suspects. Ursula Bourne is revealed to be the wife of Ralph Paton.

3. What beyond-the-surface universal human values have changed for one or more characters in the scene? Which one of those value changes is most important and should be included in the Story Grid Spreadsheet?

Let's track the value for Ursula. Privately seeking Ralph, she finds out through the newspaper that he's been arrested.
Searching (-) to Shocked (- -)

4. The Scene Event Synthesis: What Story Event sums up the scene's on-the-surface, above-the-surface, and beyond-the-surface change? We will enter that event in the Story Grid Spreadsheet.

Poirot gives Sheppard the task of assembling the suspects. They learn that Ursula is married to Ralph.

HOW THE SCENE ABIDES BY THE FIVE COMMANDMENTS OF STORYTELLING

Inciting Incident: Causal. The piece announcing Ralph's capture has come out in the paper.

Progressive Complication: Poirot has a mysterious guest. Flora and Blunt are engaged.

Turning Point Progressive Complication: Active. Poirot commissions Sheppard to invite everyone to his house for a reunion that night.

Crisis: Irreconcilable goods choice. If the house party accepts Poirot's invitation, their secrets will come out. If they turn down Poirot's invitation, they will look suspicious.

Climax: Everyone accepts, some with protestations.

Resolution: Ursula comes to visit Poirot at Sheppard's house. He introduces her as Mrs. Ralph Paton.

NOTES

- Christie uses misdirection by weaving the beats of this scene. *Why* did Poirot send Sheppard on this mission? What was Poirot doing while Sheppard was talking with Mrs. Ackroyd? He always has a reason for his actions.
- Mrs. Ackroyd continues to provide comic relief in this scene.
- Caroline provides a wealth of Red Herrings and comic relief. Her theories include: 1) A Home Office expert is visiting Poirot. 2) Miss Russell poisoned Ackroyd and stabbed him in the neck to throw the police off.
- Convention: *Secrets*. Ursula Bourne is married to Ralph Paton.

CHAPTER 22: URSULA'S SECRET

SCENE 23

2228 words

"For a moment or two ... your faith in Hercule Poirot."

Summary: Ursula tells her story. She and Ralph met through her position at the house. They married but kept the marriage a secret per Ralph's wishes, knowing Ackroyd, his stepfather, would not approve and would not give them money. When his stepfather arranged the marriage between him and Flora, Ralph agreed to it as a business arrangement. They fought the night of the murder. She threw off her ring and hasn't seen him since. Poirot points out how bad it looks for both her and Ralph.

ANALYZING THE SCENE

STORY EVENT

A Story Event is an active change of a universal human value for one or more characters as a result of conflict (one character's desires clash with another's, or an environmental shift changes the value positively or negatively).

A Working Scene contains at least one Story Event. To determine a scene's Story Event, answer these four Socratic questions:

1. What are the characters literally doing—that is, what are their micro on-the-surface actions?

Ursula recounts her love story with Ralph.

2. What is the essential tactic of the characters—that is, what above-the-surface macro behaviors are they employing that are linked to a universal human value?

Ursula tells Ackroyd about her marriage to Ralph. Ackroyd had threatened to cut them off. Neither Ralph nor Ursula has an alibi, and they both have a motive.

3. What beyond-the-surface universal human values have changed for one or more characters in the scene? Which one of those value changes is most important and should be included in the Story Grid Spreadsheet?

Let's track the value for Ursula. She feels abandoned by her husband until she realizes his absence may be for her protection.
Abandoned (--) to Protected (+)

4. The Scene Event Synthesis: What Story Event sums up the scene's on-the-surface, above-the-surface, and beyond-the-surface change? We will enter that event in the Story Grid Spreadsheet.

Ursula recounts her marriage and fight with Ralph the day of Ackroyd's murder.

HOW THE SCENE ABIDES BY THE FIVE COMMANDMENTS OF STORYTELLING

Inciting Incident: Causal: Poirot's fake story of Ralph's arrest in the newspaper caused Ursula to come see him.

Progressive Complication: Flora and Ralph's engagement was a business arrangement.

Turning Point Progressive Complication: Revelatory. Ackroyd was killed before he had a chance to cut Ralph (and his wife Ursula) out of the will. Ralph may be staying away to protect his wife.

Crisis: Irreconcilable goods choice. Will anyone reveal Ralph's current or previous location?

Climax: No one gives up Ralph's true position. Poirot tells Ursula the newspaper story was fake.

Resolution: Poirot and Caroline comfort Ursula.

NOTES

- Ursula reveals that Ralph considers Sheppard his best friend in the village.
- Convention: *Red Herring*. Newspaper paragraph (experiment), alibis, Ralph's boots/shoes
- Convention: *Red Herring:* Ursula and Ralph will receive an inheritance from Roger Ackroyd.

CHAPTER 23: POIROT'S LITTLE REUNION
SCENE 24

3525 words

"'And now,' said Caroline, rising ... was standing in the doorway."

Summary: Sheppard gives Poirot his narrative to read, which Poirot approves. Then they take Ursula to the Larches for Poirot's "little reunion." Poirot begins his summation. He introduces Ursula Paton. He goes down the chain of evidence and alibis, revealing his theory that Ackroyd was alone at 9:30 p.m. and that the dictaphone recording was overheard. Raymond insists Ralph come forward to prove his innocence, at which point he comes out of the shadows.

ANALYZING THE SCENE

STORY EVENT

A Story Event is an active change of a universal human value for one or more characters as a result of conflict (one character's desires clash with another's, or an environmental shift changes the value positively or negatively).

A Working Scene contains at least one Story Event. To determine a scene's Story Event, answer these four Socratic questions:

1. What are the characters literally doing—that is, what are their micro on-the-surface actions?

The suspects assemble at Poirot's home. Poirot lays out the case from his point of view. Ralph, the prime suspect, appears.

2. What is the essential tactic of the characters—that is, what above-the-surface macro behaviors are they employing that are linked to a universal human value?

Poirot begins to lay out the evidence before all the suspects. The dictaphone is presented as a new clue and could change the whole timeline. Ralph appears.

3. What beyond-the-surface universal human values have changed for one or more characters in the scene? Which one of those value changes is most important and should be included in the Story Grid Spreadsheet?

Let's track the value for Poirot in the interest of justice here. He's tearing down the *illusion of the case* to rebuild it truthfully.
Falsehood Masquerading as Truth (--) to Truth (+)

4. The Scene Event Synthesis: What Story Event sums up the scene's on-the-surface, above-the-surface, and beyond-the-surface change? We will enter that event in the Story Grid Spreadsheet.

Ralph shows up at Poirot's reunion.

HOW THE SCENE ABIDES BY THE FIVE COMMANDMENTS OF STORYTELLING

Inciting Incident: Causal. All the suspects assemble at the Larches at 9:00 p.m.

Turning Point Progressive Complication: Revelatory. Ackroyd had, in fact, bought a dictaphone that week (contrary to Raymond's testimony).

Crisis: Irreconcilable goods choice. Will Ralph come forward having heard the case against him, or will he continue to hide?

Climax: Ralph steps out of the shadows.

Resolution: Cliffhanger

NOTES

- The summation takes place exactly one week after Mr. Ackroyd's murder. Poirot knows the murder had already occurred by 9 p.m. on the previous Friday, 17 September. The timeline is very easy to follow.
- The case against Ralph looks convincing. However, Christie has introduced a blip of suspicion against the likable Raymond. Perhaps his being so likable this whole time has been a Red Herring. Perhaps he knew about and set up the dictaphone and used a conversation with Blunt to create a phony alibi. The attentive reader, though thrown into chaos by the sudden appearance of Ralph, will hold on to this bit of info heading into the next scene as Ralph will either defend or incriminate himself.

CHAPTER 24: RALPH PATON'S STORY
SCENE 25

1164 words

"It was a very uncomfortable ... Inspector Raglan in the morning."

Summary: Ralph tells his side of the story. Sheppard *did* find him the night after Ackroyd's death and persuaded him to hide in a nursing home to protect Ursula from suspicion. Ralph has no solid alibi for the night of the murder. Poirot challenges the murderer to step forward to save Ralph from condemnation. When he gets no response, a telegram arrives, sealing the case against the murderer. Poirot will take the clue to the police the next day. He dismisses the people in the room.

ANALYZING THE SCENE

STORY EVENT

94

A Story Event is an active change of a universal human value for one or more characters as a result of conflict (one character's desires clash with another's, or an environmental shift changes the value positively or negatively).

A Working Scene contains at least one Story Event. To determine a scene's Story Event, answer these four Socratic questions:

1. What are the characters literally doing—that is, what are their micro on-the-surface actions?

Ralph tells his story.

2. What is the essential tactic of the characters—that is, what above-the-surface macro behaviors are they employing that are linked to a universal human value?

Sheppard reveals he knew where Ralph was all along. Poirot has finished his summation. The smoking gun clue arrives. He knows the identity of the murderer without doubt. Poirot threatens to expose the murderer.

3. What beyond-the-surface universal human values have changed for one or more characters in the scene? Which one of those value changes is most important and should be included in the Story Grid Spreadsheet?

Sheppard is uncomfortable (to say the least) at the beginning of the scene when Ralph shows up; he starts scrambling when Poirot wags his finger at him. Forcing the criminal out of comfort and into "scrambling" mode is a positive for the investigator. Let's track the value for Poirot.
Suspicion (+) to Proof (++)

4. The Scene Event Synthesis: What Story Event sums up the scene's on-the-surface, above-the-surface, and beyond-the-surface change? We will enter that event in the Story Grid Spreadsheet.

Ralph proclaims his innocence as Poirot receives a telegram confirming Sheppard's guilt.

HOW THE SCENE ABIDES BY THE FIVE COMMANDMENTS OF STORYTELLING

Inciting Incident: Causal. Poirot calls Sheppard out for hiding a secret.

Turning Point Progressive Complication: Revelatory. Sheppard confesses that he convinced Ralph, after the murder, to hide out.

Crisis: Best bad choice. Will the killer confess to save Ralph? Will Poirot have to out him or her?

Climax: No one speaks up. The smoking gun clue arrives.

Resolution: Poirot dismisses the people in the room except Sheppard.

NOTES

- This is the Turning Point Progressive Complication of the Ending Payoff. The reader has been expecting this since Ralph disappeared. We needed to hear his story to pay off the beginning hook turning point promise.
- The startling revelation that Sheppard hid Paton fans into flame that spark of distrust for our narrator that arose back at Flora's revelation (chapter 7, scene 8) that he went to the Three Boars without telling us. Christie has misdirected us from that indiscretion by tying him to Poirot as his right-hand man through the middle build.
- The lines of dialogue between Poirot, Ralph, and Sheppard as they discuss how Sheppard arranged Ralph's hiding place is brilliant. Ralph talks up Sheppard's loyalty. Poirot makes cryptic jabs at Sheppard, who reveals only the truth that makes him look good. Poirot expertly steers the conversation back to Ralph's story. It's always order and method for Poirot,

and there ought to be an order to revealing clues in any mystery. Give an inch and then redirect backward.

- Poirot's reveal is a little dramatic. He claimed several times through the story that he knew everything; but did he really know before the telegram arrived?
- Poirot receives the *Smoking Gun Clue* that will seal the evidence against Sheppard—a wireless message from Sheppard's unnamed American patient.
- Convention: *Clock*. "The truth goes to Inspector Raglan in the morning!"

CHAPTER 25: THE WHOLE TRUTH
SCENE 26

2185 words

"A slight gesture from Poirot ... police. In fact—Sheppard!"

Summary: Poirot describes the murderer based on the evidence and testimonies, and then he accuses Sheppard.

ANALYZING THE SCENE

STORY EVENT

A Story Event is an active change of a universal human value for one or more characters as a result of conflict (one character's desires clash with another's, or an environmental shift changes the value positively or negatively).

A Working Scene contains at least one Story Event. To determine a scene's Story Event, answer these four Socratic questions:

1. What are the characters literally doing—that is, what are their micro on-the-surface actions?

Poirot identifies the murderer.

2. What is the essential tactic of the characters—that is, what above-the-surface macro behaviors are they employing that are linked to a universal human value?

Poirot reveals the identity of the murderer and accuses him.

3. What beyond-the-surface universal human values have changed for one or more characters in the scene? Which one of those value changes is most important and should be included in the Story Grid Spreadsheet?

Poirot has identified the murderer, and the scene resolves with an accusation. The murderer is exposed—negative for him, positive for justice and Poirot.
Theory (+) to Fact (++)

4. The Scene Event Synthesis: What Story Event sums up the scene's on-the-surface, above-the-surface, and beyond-the-surface change? We will enter that event in the Story Grid Spreadsheet.

Poirot accuses Sheppard.

HOW THE SCENE ABIDES BY THE FIVE COMMANDMENTS OF STORYTELLING

Inciting Incident: Causal. Poirot gestures for Sheppard to stay behind when the others leave.

Progressive Complication: Poirot solves the puzzle of the mysterious phone call, the moved chair, the missing dictaphone, and the shoe prints on the windowsill.

Turning Point Progressive Complication: Revelatory. At 9:30 p.m., Ackroyd was already dead. The dictaphone was playing Ackroyd's voice when it was heard later.

Crisis: Best bad choice. Should Poirot accuse Sheppard directly or go to the police?

Climax: Poirot accuses Sheppard.

Resolution: Cliffhanger

NOTES

- The logic behind the puzzle: The murderer was 1) A person on the scene straightaway; 2) "A person carrying a receptacle into which the dictaphone might be fitted" for example a doctor's bag; 3) Someone with mechanical knowledge [time lock on the dictaphone]; 4) Someone who had opportunity to take Paton's shoes from him that day and wear his shoes to the house; 5) Had an opportunity to take the dagger; 6) Had the room to himself as Parker called the police. This may be where you want to start as you map out your antagonist.
- Obligatory moment: *Exposure of the Criminal.* The global climax and the core event of Crime Story, we now know Sheppard is the murderer. Poirot confronts him without delivering him to the police.
- Convention: *Clues.* The telephone call was made to ensure the crime was discovered the night of, not next day. The chair was pulled out to obscure something from view.
- Convention: *Red Herrings:* 1) Footprints were left on the windowsill. 2) Breadcrumb back in chapter 19 about Kent's boots dropping "clean off him" incriminated Kent, but the boots were actually irrelevant. 3) Poirot's investigation of the *color* of the boots was a ruse to determine if Ralph wore shoes or boots that night.

- Convention: *Scapegoat/Prime Suspect*: Sheppard incriminated Ralph and did not protect him.

CHAPTER 26: AND NOTHING BUT THE TRUTH

SCENE 27

1063 words

"There was a dead silence ... passed out of the room."

Summary: Poirot sums up Sheppard's plan, actions, motive, and coverup, revealing why he suspected him. Poirot urges Sheppard to take another form of justice—to kill himself—instead of confessing to the police, in order to save his sister. He also urges Sheppard to finish his manuscript with full confession.

ANALYZING THE SCENE

STORY EVENT

A Story Event is an active change of a universal human value for one or more characters as a result of conflict (one character's desires clash with another's, or an environmental shift changes the value positively or negatively).

A Working Scene contains at least one Story Event. To determine a scene's Story Event, answer these four Socratic questions:

1. What are the characters literally doing—that is, what are their micro on-the-surface actions?

Poirot lays out the case against Sheppard.

2. What is the essential tactic of the characters—that is, what above-the-surface macro behaviors are they employing that are linked to a universal human value?

Poirot gives Sheppard two options for justice to prevail.

3. What beyond-the-surface universal human values have changed for one or more characters in the scene? Which one of those value changes is most important and should be included in the Story Grid Spreadsheet?

Let's track the value for Sheppard. He has been accused and now cornered as the criminal. On a global level for justice, this is a positive to a super-positive.

Accused (+) to Cornered (++)

4. The Scene Event Synthesis: What Story Event sums up the scene's on-the-surface, above-the-surface, and beyond-the-surface change? We will enter that event in the Story Grid Spreadsheet.

Poirot gives Sheppard two options for justice to prevail.

HOW THE SCENE ABIDES BY THE FIVE COMMANDMENTS OF STORYTELLING

Inciting Incident: Causal. Poirot accuses Sheppard (previous scene).

Progressive Complication: Sheppard blackmailed Mrs. Ferrars. The telegram revealed Sheppard's American patient made the mysterious call.

Turning Point Progressive Complication: Active. Poirot encourages Sheppard to take his own life—to enact justice and spare his sister the shame.

Crisis: Best bad choice. Will Sheppard confess, deny, or try to silence Poirot?

Climax: Sheppard denies his guilt.

Resolution: Sheppard leaves.

NOTES

- Convention: *Clock*. Poirot gives Sheppard an ultimatum. The next day the truth goes to Raglan unless Sheppard kills himself.
- Obligatory Moment: *Discover of the MacGuffin*. We now know Sheppard is the blackmailer and that he killed for the letter, which he burned.

CHAPTER 27: APOLOGIA

SCENE 28

872 words

"Five a.m. I am very ... here to grow vegetable marrows."

Summary: Sheppard fills in the gaps in Poirot's summation and bids adieu. He has finished his manuscript, mailed it to Poirot, and will overdose on Veronal.

ANALYZING THE SCENE

STORY EVENT

A Story Event is an active change of a universal human value for one or more characters as a result of conflict (one character's desires clash with another's, or an environmental shift changes the value positively or negatively).

A Working Scene contains at least one Story Event. To determine a scene's Story Event, answer these four Socratic questions:

1. What are the characters literally doing—that is, what are their micro on-the-surface actions?

Sheppard finishes the manuscript as confession of guilt and prepares to kill himself.

2. What is the essential tactic of the characters—that is, what above-the-surface macro behaviors are they employing that are linked to a universal human value?

Sheppard takes responsibility for his crimes.

3. What beyond-the-surface universal human values have changed for one or more characters in the scene? Which one of those value changes is most important and should be included in the Story Grid Spreadsheet?

Let's track the value for Poirot. This is the resolution of justice. *Indictment (+) to Justice (++)*

4. The Scene Event Synthesis: What Story Event sums up the scene's on-the-surface, above-the-surface, and beyond-the-surface change? We will enter that event in the Story Grid Spreadsheet.

Sheppard finishes the manuscript and prepares to kill himself.

HOW THE SCENE ABIDES BY THE FIVE COMMANDMENTS OF STORYTELLING

Inciting Incident: Causal. Sheppard finishes his manuscript.

Turning Point Progressive Complication: Sheppard confesses everything.

Crisis: Talk about best bad choice! Will Sheppard take Poirot's way out or confess to save Ralph and ruin his sister?

Climax: Sheppard selects the drug Veronal as his way out.

Resolution: Justice is served. Poirot and Raglan will discreetly handle the truth, and Ralph will be freed.

NOTES

- "All along I've had a premonition of disaster—from the moment I saw Ralph and Mrs. Ferrars with their heads together." This harkens back to the second chapter and reveals Sheppard's true motives for catching up with Ralph and Ackroyd. We now see premeditation as early as the second scene. Now we can see a whole different story playing out *off the page* through much of the beginning hook. While the on-page beginning hook involves the lay of the land, introducing characters, and finally committing the crime, Sheppard's tactics off the page are to plot the murder and incriminate Ralph.
- Obligatory Moment: *Speech in Praise of the Villain*. Sheppard gives his own speech. His motive as a narrator is revealed. "A strange end to my manuscript. I meant it to be published some day as the history of Poirot's failures!" We see another note of confidence: "I am rather pleased with myself as a writer."
- Sheppard calls it "poetic justice" to take his life by the same method Mrs. Ferrars used. Poirot and Raglan will be discreet, and Ralph will be set free. Poirot seems to be the most concerned with the common good here. He wants to exonerate Ralph, spare Caroline the shame of her brother's arrest, and still restore justice to their little town.
- Christie's innovation of the Watson character in this story is nothing short of brilliant. *The reader actually attaches to the killer since we spend more time with the narrator than the victim.*

We end up wishing for a third option for Sheppard! It's hard even to write down that the story ends super-positively since it has such a morbid end for the character we are most attached to. However, justice is the value at stake, and justice has been served.

- We learn in the very last scenes that all along, the narrator has been the most informed on the crime, more than Poirot and certainly more than the reader. Christie employs the narrative drive of mystery (reader and protagonist are in the dark) until Poirot figures out the crime, and suspense when Poirot (protagonist) has solved the mystery but is laying the trap for the narrator.
- Gap in the perfect crime: Parker noticed the chair moved. Sheppard didn't count on that. With the Master Detective subgenre, the criminal often commits an error in the perfect crime that only the Master Detective notices.
- Obligatory Moment: *Brought to Justice*. Sheppard chooses to confess, record the truth for Poirot and Raglan, and take his life in an effort to return order to King's Abbot and spare his sister.
- Talk about a satisfying genre-abiding and innovative Story. That's the definition of a Masterwork.

ABOUT THE AUTHOR

Sophie Thomas is a Story Grid Certified Editor specializing in Murder Mystery. She wrote the *Story Grid Edition to The Murder of Roger Ackroyd* and a handful of articles for Story Grid to help Murder Mystery writers better understand the stories they love and bring evolution to the genre. She believes Story Grid writers will create the evergreen sellers of the future. As an editor, Sophie has found joy in helping writers level up their craft, develop confidence through new tools, and connect more deeply to their genre and other writers. Now at home raising book-lovers, Sophie is enjoying a season of reviving her own imagination through the wonder of her three sons. Connect with Sophie online at sophiebthomas.com.

ABOUT THE EDITOR

Jay Peters is a journalist in Portland who lives with his wife. In his free time, he likes to go on runs and play games with friends and family.

Made in the USA
Columbia, SC
07 May 2021

36947753R00088